Anglican
Diversity

Anglican Diversity

Challenges for the 21st Century

Patricia Bays

ABC Publishing
ANGLICAN BOOK CENTRE

Published 2001 by
Anglican Book Centre
600 Jarvis Street
Toronto, Ontario M4Y 2J6

Canadian Cataloguing in Publication Data
Bays, Patricia
   Anglican diversity : challenges for the 21st century

ISBN 1-55126-327-0

1. Anglican Church of Canada. 2. Church and minorities.
3. Anglican Church of Canada — Doctrines. I. Title.

BX5005.B39 2001   283'.71   C2001-900867-8

Contents

Acknowledgements   7
Introduction   9

Chapter One: The Strange Land   15
Chapter Two: The Anglican Church — Yesterday and
      Today   22
Chapter Three: The Lord's Song   31
Chapter Four: Looking to the Future in Worship   47
Chapter Five: Looking to the Future in Ministry   69
Chapter Six: Social and Ethical Issues   84
Chapter Seven: Living with People of Other Denominations
      and Faiths   91
Chapter Eight: Authority in the Anglican Communion   101

Conclusion: What Is the Future of the Anglican
   Communion?   112
Appendix: A Response to the 1998 Lambeth Conference
   of Bishops   124
Bibliography   126

Acknowledgements

This book is based on two sets of addresses: the Martin Memorial lectures entitled "The Compass Rose: Flowering or Fading?", given at the College of Emmanuel and St. Chad in Saskatoon in May 1999, and three addresses on the theme "Composing the Lord's Song," given at the diocese of Calgary's "Theology Alive" weekend in October 1999. I want to thank both those groups for the honour of being invited to address them. It was a joy to explore with them the topic of Anglican identity at this time in our history.

My thanks to those who provided inspiration and encouragement for the writing of the book, particularly Bishop Mark Dyer of Virginia Theological Seminary, with whom I shared the platform at "Theology Alive," and Fredrica Harris Thompsett of the Episcopal Divinity School. Much of the book was written in the library of St. Paul University, Ottawa, and I am grateful for access to that excellent collection of resources. Thank you also to publisher Robert Maclennan, editor Greig Dunn, and the publishing staff of the Anglican Book Centre for their work on the manuscript.

A special thank-you to my family — to my husband, Eric, who has a deep interest in and love for the Anglican Church and whose encouragement and support make possible all that I do in the church, and to our son Jonathan and daughter Rebecca, whose encouragement and good humour keep us from taking ourselves too seriously.

Introduction

Anglicans in recent years, troubled by divisions over many issues in the church, have been forced to ask themselves: What constitutes Anglicanism? By what authority does the church make decisions? The spread of Anglicanism to many parts of the world, and the resultant diversity of customs and canons, has given both an urgency and a sharp edge to discussion of these perennial questions. Each province of the Anglican Communion is autonomous and makes laws to govern its own life. While provinces consult together, none is bound by the decisions of others. We are thus a communion with a wide variety of customs and a wide variety of theological emphases.

We are now asking: How much diversity can there be before Anglicanism falls apart? Are there limits to Anglican diversity? How do we define these limits? Though we are seeing a wide range of Anglican customs and practices — here in Canada as well as elsewhere — we are also seeing an increasing polarization of opinion between conservatives and liberals in our church. This polarization focuses the question of diversity for us in an immediate way.

I am disturbed by a number of recent books and addresses that present a gloomy picture of a divided Anglicanism, and that forecast the death of the Anglican Communion and the breakdown of the Anglican Church into conservative and liberal factions. I recognize that we are living in changing and difficult times. But living with diversity is essential to Anglican identity, and I want to give a hopeful picture of the future of Anglicanism. Our diversity is our strength. It enables us to be an effective Christian witness in a world that is itself characterized by ambiguity and diversity.

I believe that Anglicanism is characterized by a distinctive way of doing theology. And I believe that a tolerance for diversity is an integral part of being Anglican. So I believe that our current struggles and debates are essential to being who we are, and I am hopeful that our diversity will strengthen us as we respond to God's call to be part of the church, the body of Christ. In *Anglican Diversity*, I will articulate a foundation for this belief, then explore how such an Anglican identity can help us to respond to the challenges of the twenty-first century.

Composing

During the planning for Calgary's "Theology Alive" conference, there was some discussion about taking the words of Psalm 137, "How shall we sing the Lord's song in a strange land?", and putting a new twist on them by speaking of "composing the Lord's song" or of "composing a life together." This intriguing idea seemed to me to give the phrase a more dynamic meaning.

The word *compose* means to put together, to bring together various elements to form a whole. It has to do with action, with change, with shaping and creating from different "component" parts. I like to think we are composing the Lord's song as well as singing it. When we compose, we not only sing the song but we create it. We bring together different notes and phrases, different melodies, to bring to birth something new. Out of our own experience, and out of the experience of others, we create a new song.

Some years ago I read a book called *Composing a Life* by Mary Catherine Bateson, who tells the story of several women and their struggle to fashion their lives out of the different strands of family and work and leisure. The first chapter examines the theme of composing a life, and it suggested some interesting insights.

Bateson begins by reflecting on the difficulties of composing a life in today's fragmented and divided society — in "the strange land," as we have called it.

> In a stable society, composing a life is somewhat like throwing a pot or building a house in a traditional form: the materials are known, the hands move skilfully in tasks familiar from thousands of performances, the fit of the completed whole in the common life is understood ...

> Today, the materials and skills from which a life is composed are no longer clear. It is no longer possible to follow the path of previous generations ... Our lives not only take new directions; they are subject to repeated redirection ... Many of the most basic concepts we use to construct a sense of self or the design of a life have changed their meanings: Work. Home. Love. Commitment.[1]

---

1 Mary Catherine Bateson, *Composing a Life* (New York: Atlantic Monthly Press, 1989), ch. 1, pp. 1–2.

In today's strange land we are creating a new entity from diverse and sometimes contradictory elements — trying to bring into being a harmony from different strands and traditions.

Bateson speaks of the importance of improvisation, which she describes as combining "familiar and unfamiliar components in response to new situations."[2] Musicians, for example, compose new tunes or variations on old tunes in response to the spirit of the moment. Dancers do the same. Experienced cooks improvise as they take old recipes and adapt them to the ingredients at hand. A quilter combines the material from the scrap basket to make a patchwork quilt out of the odds and ends. Life today means adapting to changing circumstances, improvising as we go along — in Bateson's words, making "something coherent from conflicting elements."

But there must be something that holds the improvisation together, that keeps the disparate and changing elements connected and harmonious in the whole composition. Improvisation is not random; it is a process of interweaving and integration that has an underlying order. In music, there is a key signature, a rhythmic pattern, a resolution of chords.

So it is the Lord's song that holds together our composition in the strange land. This song is the record of God's actions in history. It is the gospel of Jesus Christ. It is the tradition of the teaching of the church. It is the ongoing revelation of God in contemporary life. All of these provide the underlying pattern in which our new song is grounded. Without this foundation, our song becomes a series of disconnected fragments. When

---

2   *Ibid.*, p. 3.

C. S. Lewis describes the creation of the land of Narnia, he has Aslan the lion, the figure of Christ, create the world by singing it into being. Aslan creates as he composes. Composing means that we take an active part in shaping the music rather than simply repeating it or even interpreting it. We create out of diverse elements when we compose.

In the church, we are composing the Lord's song in difficult times. The church contains members with very different views. The church is challenged by the need to explore complex ethical and theological issues. We face the challenge of taking all these strands and traditions and weaving them into a strong harmonious whole. We weave the traditions of the past into the circumstances of the present. We weave together many different stories and many different experiences. Complexity is a given, but it need not mean fragmentation.

Two kinds of composing are going on. Individual Christians struggle to understand the faith and their place in it. And the church, as a corporate body, also struggles to compose a new and faithful song for our times. Tensions and divisions challenge us to work with other Anglicans and with other Christians to understand and to live the Christian faith. That faith, the faith "that was once for all entrusted to the saints" (Jude 3), is a dynamic and living faith. God is continually revealing Godself in new ways, times, and places. As Bateson has said, "Our visions are not fixed, but emergent."

Chapter 1 of *Anglican Diversity* begins with the present, by looking at the strange land: the society in which we live, the culture in which we are called to preach the gospel. What is it like? Where does it cause difficulties for us as Christians? How does it shape and influence us?

Chapter 2 looks at the church, the place where many of us spend much of our time, where we find a home. Where do we experience difficulties and conflicts today in our life in the Anglican Church? What does our history teach us about living with conflict? Our present struggles with ambiguity and diversity seem to have been with us for a long time.

Is there a distinctively Anglican approach to theology that enables us to sing the Lord's song in a divided world? That is the question asked in chapter 3. I believe that there is a distinctively Anglican way of doing theology, a particular set of lenses through which we view the revelation of God in Jesus Christ. It is important to hold up Anglicanism's affirming and incarnational theology in a time when much popular Christianity seems to speak of a dark and punishing theology.

In chapters 4 through 7, we look at some of the issues facing Anglicans today — forms of worship, forms of ministry, difficult social and ethical issues, and concerns such as ecumenism and interfaith dialogue, which arise in our multicultural and multifaith society.

Finally, in chapter 8, we look at issues of authority and how authority is defined by Anglicans.

The conclusion focuses on on the future of the Anglican Communion. The Compass Rose is a symbol of the communion. Is that rose flowering or fading? I believe that reports of our demise are premature. I believe that our theology embraces diversity as a response to the Good News of God in Jesus Christ. This emphasis allows us to respond to the needs of a diverse and complex world.

CHAPTER ONE

The Strange Land

The world we live in

We are living at the end of a century of profound change. My husband's mother died in March 1998, one month short of her 101st birthday. It astonishes her family to think of the changes she saw in her lifetime. Born in 1897 in England during the reign of Queen Victoria, she lived through the reigns of six monarchs. She saw the invention of the motor car, the airplane, radio, and television. She began raising five children without labour-saving appliances such as the electric stove, the washer and dryer. In later life, she had a microwave and a VCR, enjoyed air travel, kept in touch with family and friends by phone and letter. From the horse and carriage to the first flight of the Wright brothers in 1903, and to the 1969 Apollo moon landing, her world changed dramatically.

In fast-paced North America, we are overwhelmed by so many options that it is tempting to try them all. Should we do fitness classes, yoga, Tai Chi, aerobics, swimming? Should the children take up hockey, ballet, gymnastics, music? This richness of opportunity is often alienating, pulling us away from close contact with our families and friends. As a consequence, although we are busier and see more people in the course of a day than ever, we often feel more alone. Add to this the demands of work that may require us to pull up roots and move, and the lure of more open space and lower house prices in the suburbs, and it is easy to see why most of us have never known the support of the extended family of grandparents, aunts and uncles, and cousins. Each small family is on its own for support and comfort.

Our life is rich in technology. The computer, that relatively recent invention, now intrudes into and influences most aspects of our lives. Few of us had personal computers twenty years ago; now many of us regard word processing and e-mail as essential to our lives. Computer chips and engineering skills provide us with machines that are supposed to save time and labour but may well have the opposite effect. Having the whole world of information at our fingertips overwhelms us with data and demands our time and attention to make sense of it. We have less time than ever for ourselves and our families.

The new technologies confront us with complex ethical issues. Reproductive technologies and developments in medicines and treatments pose questions about the creation and prolongation of life that we have not had to face before: surrogate motherhood, assisted suicide, contraception, abortion, organ transplants, genetic engineering, cloning.

We live in a time of economic upheaval. We seem to be witnessing the death of the family farm in many parts of Canada. The fisheries are dying. Retail empires have crumbled. Jobs are lost in all sectors. Even people in management, used to a secure income to pay for the mortgage, two cars, and vacation travel, now find themselves unemployed, and PhD's may spend their whole lives working on the basis of temporary contracts. The rich are getting richer and the poor, poorer.

Violence has gained a new prominence in Canadian society. We know the horror of schoolyard killings, shootouts in the street, date rape, muggings. The Canada that took for granted the Christian faith and many of its social and moral consequences is no more.

The unknown story

The Christian story, which we call the Judaeo-Christian tradition, once formed and shaped Western European and North American culture. The scriptures, Christian symbolism, and a common ethical teaching shaped literature, music, art, and social policy.

Forty years ago professors of literature could assume that students would identify symbols and biblical references in order to build an interpretation of a poem or a novel. A few years ago a friend who teaches English at the University of Regina told me that he was teaching Milton's sonnet "On His Blindness" to a first-year class. He read the line, "And that one talent which is death to hide," and asked, "What does this image mean?" Out of a class of thirty students in their late teens or early twenties, there was not one who had heard the parable of the talents.

When I was an arts student at Trinity College in the early 1960s, all students in all disciplines were required to take a religious knowledge course for each of their four years. These ranged from introductory courses on the Bible and Christian doctrine to courses on Christian existentialism and world religions. Theological study was taken seriously as a respectable university discipline, part of the mainstream of study, and not as a specialty reserved for those preparing for ordained ministry. I have heard from classmates (now in academic teaching and not necessarily active participants in the life of the church) who say that these courses were among the most important of their academic preparation because they provided the tools to understand literature and culture. Our current leaders of business and government, journalists and writers, were shaped by a religious education.

All this has changed. University education is almost entirely secular, and many academics regard theology as unsuitable for inclusion in the university. Public schools no longer have Christmas pageants, so even this basic Christian story is not widely known; in fact, there have been efforts to eradicate the use of the word *Christmas* in schools and to substitute *winter holiday*. Since church attendance has declined drastically, fewer and fewer Canadians have been formed by the stories of the faith. The basic tools for interpreting the culture of previous ages are missing, so that culture shaped by the Christian faith is not accessible without deliberate study.

The Christian church in the Middle Ages founded hospitals and schools. It undertook social programs such as caring for the poor and feeding the hungry. In later centuries the church battled against slavery, child labour, and the slum conditions of large cities, and for universal education, affordable health care, and programs to help the disadvantaged. The church spoke out on such issues and helped to set laws and standards. But the church has been sidelined. Governments and secular charities have taken over much of the social programming: health care, education, shelter for the homeless, food banks for the hungry. Yet the church still attempts to make its voice heard on social policy and is occasionally successful. As governments have slashed spending on social programs, the churches, along with voluntary agencies, have taken up the slack. When the issue of capital punishment came up for debate in the House of Commons a few years ago, the churches acting together may have turned the tide of public opinion so that the ban on capital punishment was upheld. Today the church's plea for forgiveness of the debt of developing nations is having an influence.

Nevertheless, in a society based on values that exalt wealth, power, science, and technology, ignorance of the meaning and implications of the Christian story is so deep and widespread that many people can make no sense out of the church's actions. A few years ago in Regina, local leaders of major Christian denominations held a press conference to speak on the issue of gambling, a social concern linked with poverty, job loss, addiction, child neglect, domestic upheaval, and exploitation of those with low incomes. Following the presentation, a reporter asked my husband, then the diocesan bishop, why the church would have any interest in the issue of gambling. The reporter seemed genuinely puzzled by the involvement of church leaders in what seemed to be an economic matter.

The fact remains that the church is, and must be, deeply involved with what goes on in society. The God who chose to be born as a human being and lead a human life cares for humans and the lives they lead. Society is the natural sphere of action for Christians. We are not called out of the world to leave it behind and join God in some distant heavenly realm; we are called to take responsibility for our social, economic, and political order. We are called to ensure that human society is just and welcoming to all people.

Signs of hope in the church today

Christians have been used to living together with other Christians in our neighbourhoods, at our jobs, at our schools, and yet worshipping at different churches on Sunday along with others of our own ethnic background, language, and culture. In more recent years, however, the pressure many of us feel from an increasingly secular society has been leading us to consider our similarities as well as our differences and to work together in service to the community.

Moreover, in multicultural multifaith Canada, we live side by side with people of myriad cultures and world religions. Toronto, for example, has been designated by the United Nations as the most multicultural city in the world. Rather than simply trying to convert non-Christians directly to our faith, we have begun to enter into dialogue with them in a spirit of understanding and acceptance.

In secular society, we have many allies: people who are working to save the biosphere from harm and total destruction; people who champion causes of social justice such as providing homes for the homeless and food for the hungry; people who are campaigning to maintain good and affordable universal health care and education. The newspapers are full of stories of the concern of human beings for each other. *Ordinary Grace*, a recent popular book by Kathleen A. Brehony, is subtitled: *An examination of the roots of compassion, altruism, and empathy, and the ordinary individuals who help others in extraordinary ways.* Science and new technologies make us more capable than ever before of responding to each other's needs.

One more development should be of special interest to the church. All around us there is deep spiritual hunger. Surveys show that most people still believe in God. Bookstores are filled with books about the spiritual quest. Meditation classes are widely advertised in newspapers, even on telephone poles. People are asking big questions about meaning and significance. How can the church respond?

CHAPTER TWO

The Anglican Church
— Yesterday and Today

Among the most notable characteristics of Anglicanism are
its wide range of customs and practices, and its historic
tolerance for diversity and ambiguity. Yet today in the church
we sense a breakdown in tolerance in the polarization of opinion between conservatives and liberals. Conservative
Anglo-Catholics line up with conservative evangelicals and
charismatics to protest the liberal positions taken by other
members of the church. Liberals push for change in areas related to social justice, theological interpretation, and moral
issues, and they encourage more experimentation in language
and liturgy.

Increasingly in the Anglican Church of Canada, major issues threaten to divide us. Debate over forms of worship and
language seems to have cooled for the moment, but heated debate continues over the ethics of medical technology and issues
of human sexuality. Debate is opening on new forms of ministry, especially in parishes with declining numbers and resources.
Legal challenges related to residential schools for aboriginal
people will set the agenda for church meetings for many years
in the future, and the financial implications of legal decisions
will challenge us to find news ways of maintaining parish and

diocesan life. Behind all of these issues lies a debate about the authority of scripture and the interpretation of the Bible in our present time and culture. How do we arrive at the deeper truth behind the literal words of scripture?

Anglican diversity is not new

The 1998 Lambeth Conference was faced with the question of where the limits lay to tolerance of diversity in the Anglican Communion. Anglicanism spread to many parts of the world, following the movement of the British Empire. In each country, the Anglican Church put down roots and adapted the traditional English services to reflect the language and customs of the local area. Each began to look a bit different from Anglican churches in other countries. Today Anglicans are part of a worldwide family of thirty-eight independent churches, each with its own language and music and customs but linked together by our historic descent from the church in England, our prayer books, our customs and traditions, our form of government, and a characteristic way of doing theology.

Because each province is autonomous, we now find within the Anglican Communion a wide variety of practice. How much variety is too much? Do we have enough in common to continue to call ourselves Anglicans, and to recognize others of different views as being part of the Anglican family? I want to affirm strongly that I am hopeful about the future of the Anglican Church. There is much in our history and in our distinctive way of doing theology that has helped us to survive and to grow through periods of division.

A look at our history may help to prepare us for living in a time of opposing viewpoints. Consider these quotations as a reminder of the difficulties we have had in defining Anglican identity and the struggles we have had in embracing new ideas:

We will not receive this service because it is but a Christmas game. *(Words from the uprising in Cornwall protesting the radical new Book of Common Prayer, 1549)*

The Church has authority to establish that for an order at one time which at another time it may abolish, and in both do well. *(Richard Hooker, sixteenth century)*

There is no doubt that we are passing through a period of unsettlement in religious beliefs. *(Bishop Charles Gore, 1907, as the church grappled with the implications of the "new science" and the writing of Charles Darwin)*

The attempt to draw lines and fix limits, though no doubt it is sometimes necessary, is always fraught with danger. In England, and especially in the English Church, it has always proven a complete failure. *(The Very Rev. W. H. Hutton, Dean of Winchester, 1926)*

The Church of England has an exceedingly chaotic system of truth. *(The Bishop of Zanzibar, 1929)*

These discussions about the limits of Anglican diversity clearly have been with us for a long time and will no doubt remain with us. For ours is a church whose modern form was born in a climate of religious dissent, and it has often tried to steer a middle course among a variety of points of view.

Our history

The fifteenth and sixteenth centuries in Europe were times of change and upheaval in church and society. New translations of scripture into local languages gave a renewed understanding of early Christian teaching, and discontent with papal government and abuses of church customs led to doctrinal and organizational reform in Europe. In England, William Tyndale translated the Bible into English. But King Henry VIII was conservative in theology and practice, and was rewarded by the pope with the title "Defender of the Faith" for his writing against Martin Luther.

It was the political difficulties around the succession to the throne, and the wish for a strong monarchy to preserve England's sovereignty from domination by foreign powers, that led Henry to remove the church in England from the control of the pope. The Church of England, constituted by act of Parliament, was at first little different from the Catholic Church *in* England except for the matter of allegiance to the pope. Before long, however, theologians trained in Lutheran and Calvinist theology began to influence the English church. A party that favoured reform gained increasing influence with the king; as a result, many liturgical practices were abolished, all the monasteries were dissolved, and official statements were published admitting certain reformed views into the church. With the death of Henry, the reformers gained control.

The development of the *Book of Common Prayer* is a good example of the tensions of this period. Thomas Cranmer, knowledgeable about liturgical developments on the continent, combined many of the ideas he found there with contemporary English translations of the Latin Mass and Offices. The 1549 Prayer Book was a compromise between these new liturgical ideas and the old Latin texts reworked in English. Being a compromise, it pleased neither traditionalists nor reformers. Three years later, in 1552, a second *Book of Common Prayer* was issued, following more Protestant principles. For example, the Black Rubric (so-called because it was printed in black ink, unlike the other rubrics that were printed in red) appended to the service of Holy Communion, could be understood as denying any real presence of Christ in the eucharist. Government agents continued to enforce regulations requiring that altars and statutes be torn down, vestments destroyed, and the old service books burned.

After the reign of Mary I, during which time the church was returned to the Roman obedience, the new government of Elizabeth I issued the third *Book of Common Prayer* in 1559 — a mere ten years after the first book. The Black Rubric was omitted. The 1552 order of Holy Communion included words designed to deny any saving power in the sacrament beyond helping us to remember Christ's actions: "Take and eat this in remembrance that Christ died for thee, and feed on him in thy heart, by faith, with thanksgiving." But in Elizabeth's book, the 1549 words were added as well: "The body of our Lord Jesus Christ which was given for thee, preserve thy body and soul into everlasting life." These could be understood as recognizing the sacramental presence and power. Any hope of expressing one single doctrinal position on the eucharist was seen to be impossible. Subsequent prayer books maintained a similar balance of traditional and reformed positions.

Before long Anglicans were celebrating their church as a *Via Media*, a middle way between catholic and protestant, conservative and reformed positions, while continuing to search for the deeper truth in which these partial truths might be reconciled. Liturgical and theological diversity have thus been part of the life of our church since the sixteenth century.

Diversity has continued, fostered by the many movements for change in our church. The evangelical revival of the eighteenth and nineteenth centuries placed a new emphasis on personal conversion, the sole authority of scripture, and the preaching of the Word. In the nineteenth century, the Anglo-Catholic revival brought a new emphasis on the liturgical and sacramental life of the church, and looked to Christian tradition to affirm the church's catholic and apostolic nature. Both these groups helped the church to look outward, to ministry in the slums of England and to missionary work around the world, including here in Canada.

The Anglican Church continues to hold a variety of theological positions in creative tension. Evangelical Anglicans place a strong emphasis on personal conversion, on preaching, on the authority of scripture. Anglo-Catholics place a strong emphasis on sacramental worship, and on the tradition of the church. Charismatic Anglicans focus on the gifts of the Holy Spirit and prefer a more spontaneous style of worship. And within each of these strands of Anglicanism there are both conservative and liberal stances. Some Anglo-Catholics, for instance, hold a conservative view on such issues as the ordination of women while others of a more liberal mind have welcomed it.

The majority of Canadian Anglicans tend to stand on a middle ground that is nourished by a number of Anglican traditions. This was not always so. Our differences were focused much more sharply in the last century. In Canada in the mid-1800s, there were ferocious arguments over liturgy, doctrine, the content of theological education, even issues as seemingly trivial as robed choirs. In Upper Canada in this period, there were not one but two church newspapers, one high church and one low, which fueled the flames by taking sides in these debates. Missionary work was conducted by different agencies: for example, the Church Missionary Society and the Colonial and Continental Church Society — both evangelical — and the high church Society for the Propagation of the Gospel. In western Canada there were great differences in teaching, in architecture, and in patterns of worship between churches founded by each society. Even in the 1960s, theological colleges such as Emmanuel in Saskatoon and St. Chad's in Regina, Wycliffe and Trinity in Toronto, were identified as low or high church, with party lines clearly drawn. These differences have largely vanished. I grew up in a small parish in Ontario in which the Holy Communion was celebrated from the north end of the altar, with the priest standing sideways to the congregation, wearing cassock, surplice, black scarf, and academic hood. This was a mark of an extreme evangelical stance in liturgy and doctrine. It would be almost impossible to find such a church in Canada today. Our differences are in some ways much less than they were earlier in our history. Yet differences remain.

An inclusive church

Our Anglican story reminds us that we are a church shaped by a time of religious conflict, a church that continues to struggle to define itself in terms of acceptance of diversity within broad limits. We have never been able to insist on a narrow and restrictive focus. Our efforts at inclusion have challenged us, and have strengthened us to bear witness to the gospel in an uncertain world. We are wary of being drawn into a narrow and exclusive mould. As the Dean of Winchester phrased it, the attempt to draw lines and to fix limits is always fraught with danger.

An inclusive church that has learned to live together with great variety and diversity is well placed to be an instrument of the gospel in today's world of rapid change, economic dislocation, and great diversity. Our forms of church government allow for growth and change. Our liturgical tradition and our worldwide spread encourage us to find room for a variety of cultures and languages. Our approach to world relief and development in the last half of this century has produced a form of non-aggressive giving that has helped both to shape us as givers and to allow us to minister to the needs of a fragmented and hurting world.

The Anglican Communion is held together by "bonds of affection" — the goodwill of its members — rather than by legislation. We are passing through a time of change and diversity, different perhaps in subject from the debates of earlier times but not very different in the *variety* of opinions and belief. Historically Anglicans have always been able to work at building a deeper unity that has helped to overcome differences. I believe that we can preserve the life of the Anglican Communion if we work together with goodwill to explore and express what the gospel means in terms of today's complex and challenging society.

Canada's Governor General, Adrienne Clarkson, has spoken of two kinds of societies: punishing societies and forgiving societies. Such a description might well apply to the church. Should the Anglican Church be a punishing church, excluding all those who do not fit a narrow definition of membership? Or should it continue to be a forgiving church, one that welcomes and includes people of different views and experiences? The answer is clear.

CHAPTER THREE

The Lord's Song

The Lord's song that we are called to compose is the good news of God's redeeming love in Jesus Christ. God the loving Creator brings healing and wholeness to a broken world. We are called to compose this song with other Christians, as members of a choir of different voices. As Anglicans, we bring a distinctive voice to this choir, for we talk about God in a distinctive way that takes into account the complexity and ambiguity of the strange land in which we live.

A distinctive Anglican theology

Our distinctively Anglican way of doing theology is based on how we look at scripture, on our understanding of what the church is, and on our view of authority in the church.

The way Anglicanism sees the revelation of God in Jesus Christ derives from our history and from the culture in which we have grown. We are not a "confessional" church. Anglicans do not have a clearly set out document like the Augsburg Confession (Lutheran) or the Westminster Confession (Presbyterian), in which we define our theology. Nor have we been successful at setting out a systematic exposition of Anglican doctrine. The Doctrine Commission of the Church of England in 1981 said that, in their opinion, "doctrine should be authoritatively defined as little and as seldom as possible." As Anglicans we try not to lock ourselves too firmly into a set of absolute statements because we recognize that for every statement there is always another side that needs to be addressed.

Some foundational principles in the faith that we profess do of course exist. They might be summed up in a statement such as the Chicago-Lambeth Quadrilateral, proposed first by a General Convention of the Episcopal Church held in Chicago in 1886 and made a resolution at the Lambeth Conference of 1888. This statement sets out the basic principles that the Anglican Church would want to affirm in its dialogues with a view to reunion with other churches. The four principles uphold:

1. the Holy Scriptures as the "ultimate standard of faith";
2. the Apostles' Creed and the Nicene Creed as the "sufficient statement of the Christian faith";
3. the two Sacraments "ordained by Christ Himself" (baptism and the Supper of the Lord);
4. the "Historic Episcopate, locally adapted in the methods of its administration to the varying needs of the nations and peoples."

Other principles have been maintained firmly throughout our history as a denomination:

- the importance of common prayer and set forms of liturgy, which not only shape our worship but which also contain the words that describe the content of our beliefs;

- a form of church government with three orders of ordained ministry; a life organized in dioceses, each headed by a bishop; a synodical system with representative clergy and lay people joining with the bishop in the government of the church;
- an affirmation of the importance of the sacraments, recognizing that God's grace is expressed to us through material things. Baptism brings us into full membership in the church, and the eucharist is the weekly food for our journey;
- a strong belief in the goodness of God's creation and in the world as the proper sphere for God's action and ours. Anglicans hold an optimistic view of humanity — that we are part of God's good creation. We are confident that God's plan, through God's grace, is to bring us to our full potential as children of God.

When other denominations have done things differently, we have always maintained certain practices: the bishop as minister of confirmation; the priests as the only presiders at the eucharist; the reverent consumption of the bread and wine after communion.

Anglicans allow a wide exploration of the scriptures and of theology, but we do not say that belief is a matter of individual opinion. We affirm the faith of the historic creeds, while allowing freedom of exploration within the context outlined above. We affirm the standards of Scripture, Tradition, and Reason, by which we test our beliefs while tolerating a wide diversity of opinion. Our liturgical texts articulate our beliefs, and we have a commitment to seek the common mind of the church through our systems of government and of consultation.

Our style of theological discourse reflects our acceptance of the world as a place of ambiguity in which we continually explore faith in relation to the changes and challenges we meet. John Westerhoff, an Anglican priest and educator, writes in a foreword to a book by his wife, Caroline:

> While never anti-intellectual, Anglicans are more at home with the intuitive way of thinking and knowing than the intellectual. They prefer art to philosophy and are more comfortable in the world of symbol, myth and ritual than that of systematic theology. They are more at home with liturgy that makes use of the arts rather than discursive prose, because Anglicans affirm the anagogical, the metaphorical, the paradoxical, and the symbolic in the exploration of human experience. That is why some of their best theologians have been poets.[3]

In our own lifetime, our great theologians have included archbishops William Temple and Michael Ramsey; historians such as Owen and Henry Chadwick, John Booty, and Cyril Richardson; liturgical scholars such as Dom Gregory Dix, A. G. Hebert, Marion Hatchett, and Louis Weil; biblical scholars such as N. T. Wright, and Reginald Fuller, and Canadians Frank Beare, Gerald Janzen, and Terry Donaldson; scholars of Christian doctrine such as Stephen Sykes, John Macquarrie, Rowan

---

3   Caroline Westerhoff, *Calling: A Song for the Baptized* (Cambridge: Cowley Publications, 1994), pp. ix–x.

Williams, Richard Holloway, and Canadians Eugene Fairweather and Bill Crockett.

But our Anglican spirituality has also been shaped by writers of the imagination, themselves shaped by the Anglican tradition in which they lived and worshipped. Among the great writers who shape and are shaped by our distinctive way of doing theology are George Herbert; C. S. Lewis; William Shakespeare; T. S. Eliot; Christopher Fry; Madeleine L'Engle; Dorothy Sayers; and P. D. James. These writers help us to see the integration of our faith with everyday life and culture. Poetry, fiction, drama; the literature of the imagination comes easily to Anglicans. Nourished by the language of the *Book of Common Prayer*, we recognize that words are enormously important and evocative, not to be trivialized or proclaimed lightly.

Urban Holmes says much the same thing in *What Is Anglicanism?*

We Anglicans are not given to writing great theology. There are notable exceptions, but they are difficult to remember, but when Anglicanism is at its best its liturgy, its poetry, its music and its life can create a world of wonder in which it is very easy to fall in love with God.[4]

Anglican writer L. William Countryman, in *The Poetic Imagination: An Anglican Spiritual Tradition*, identifies Anglican spirituality as a conversation in which lyric poetry plays an

---

4   Urban T. Holmes III, *What Is Anglicanism?* (Toronto: Anglican Book Centre, 1982), p. 5.

important role, and he illustrates this with reference to English poets of several periods. He says,

> The very fact that this spirituality has embodied itself in poetry rather than in prose has consequences for the tradition. It encourages it to stay close to the experiential and to share itself in a conversation of equals rather than move towards issuing rules and directions and taking shape as a school in which those who know everything instruct those who know nothing.[5]

There is much that is metaphorical about Christian doctrine, for it uses words that are patient of several interpretations. Using metaphor and poetry allows us to remain open to the movement of the Holy Spirit. By not being too detailed in our definitions, we allow an ongoing conversation among a variety of voices. We encourage the exploration of a faith that is rich and complex.

Here are some of the factors that make Anglican theology particularly receptive to dealing with diversity and ambiguity.

Scripture, Tradition, and Reason

The traditional way in which we define Anglican theology is the balance among Scripture, Tradition, and Reason,

---

5 William L. Countryman, *The Poetic Imagination: An Anglican Spiritual Tradition* (Maryknoll: Orbis Books, 1999), p. 36.

which Richard Hooker articulated in the sixteenth century. Holy Scripture is a basic authority for Anglicans, but it is always to be read in the light of Tradition, the collective wisdom of the church that has been received and taught throughout the centuries.

Both Scripture and Tradition are to be examined by the light of Reason. The work of discerning God's will through Scripture and Tradition is demanding, but God has given us the gifts of reason and balanced judgement.

Some Christian denominations make the literal interpretation of scripture the supreme authority. When taken to an extreme position, we call this fundamentalism. Some churches make tradition the supreme authority: the Magisterium, the pronouncements of the church hierarchy on doctrinal issues. Some groups, such as Unitarians, make reason supreme. Anglicans have tried to hold the three in balance, even when there has been uneasy tension. For example, one of the concerns raised by some bishops who attended the Lambeth Conference in 1998 was their perception that the conference was affirming a much narrower view of the authority of scripture than Anglicans had previously done.

Anglicanism believes in bringing the best of contemporary biblical scholarship to our study of scripture. And we believe also that Tradition is always developing, as we try to understand the meaning of the gospel for our own age. English theologian George Guiver has described Tradition in this way:

> It is like the model of a DNA molecule, infuriatingly complex and many-faceted, and changing slowly as it goes along. Tradition can never be stuck. Once it is stuck,

it ceases to be Tradition and becomes a museum-piece
… the Tradition hands on to us building blocks with
which we are to build the future in our own style.[6]

He goes on to commend our reverence for Tradition but warns,
"The other side of that coin is that it belongs to reverence to
allow that which is revered to live and to change." [7] He points
out that you can only stop something growing by killing it!

Christian doctrine is dynamic, something to be explored in
the light of Scripture and Tradition under the guidance of Reason. So we Anglicans should not be frightened by diversity, but
should find ourselves comfortable in exploring the Christian
faith in all its ambiguity as part of the community of the church.

Lessons from history

Our history should be helpful to us. The Anglican Church
was formed in a period of religious and political dissension and, from its earliest times, has tried to hold together a
variety of theological positions and emphases. All our prayer
books express this diversity of views. One of our earliest and
best theologians, Richard Hooker, said,

---

6   George Guiver, *Faith in Momentum: The Distinctiveness of the
Church* (London: SPCK, 1990), p. 40.
7   *Ibid.*, pp. 41–2.

The Church has authority to establish that for an order at one time, which at another time it may abolish, and in both do well.[8]

Doctrine has never been static but is always changing and developing in new times and places. Bishop Charles Gore, writing in 1908 about *The New Theology and the Old Religion*, says,

> In such an age of religious unsettlement, it is as well to remember that, after all, it is to ages of such mental ferment as ours, and not to ages of mental stagnation, that we owe our great debts of gratitude for the works of religious construction. It was for an age of universal intellectual ferment and unsettlement that there emerged the solid structure of the catholic creeds; it was in an atmosphere of serious unsettlement that Butler and others in the eighteenth century relaid the intellectual foundation on which Wesley and Simeon and Pusey and Newman built their works of spiritual recovery. If religion is "the pearl of great price" we must not expect to win it cheaply, and intellectual trouble is no more to be resented than pain of body.[9]

Gore was writing in a time when the new science was seen as a threat to the Christian faith. But Gore goes on to say, "A living

8   Richard Hooker, *On the Laws of Ecclesiastical Polity*, Folger Library Edition, Book V. 8, Lines 17–19.
9   Charles Gore, *The New Theology and the Old Religion* (London: John Murray, 1908), p. 4.

theology must always in a sense be a new theology" and religious beliefs always need to be brought "into harmony with the thought of their time, with all truth *so far as it is known.*"[10] Our own time is certainly no exception.

Indeed, this dissension has been true not only of Anglican history but of the history of the Christian church as a whole. The Virginia Report of the Inter-Anglican Theological and Doctrinal Commission makes this point.

> From the earliest time in the history of the Christian community, an admonishing voice has been heard exhorting believers to maintain agreement with each other and thereby to avert division. From an almost equally early date they have found consensus, even on apparently major matters, singularly difficult to achieve. When the second century churches evolved a collection of early Christian documents, which came to be called the New Testament, they had a few documents which did not attest and reflect deep disagreements, and the formation of the collection itself was the product of controversies. Nevertheless the controversies themselves were stages on a road towards greater consensus.[11]

Christian doctrine is the product of controversy and is continually being reshaped in response to new situations. A living theology clearly must always be a new theology.

---

10 *Ibid.*, p. 19.
11 The Virginia Report of the Inter-Anglican Theological and Doctrinal Commision, in *Being Anglican in the Third Millenium* (Harrisburg: Morehouse, 1997), p. 231.

The Incarnation

Anglican theology is deeply rooted in the doctrine of the Incarnation. We believe that God created the world in all its diversity, and saw that the world was good. We believe that in Jesus, God chose to become human and to share our human life. Bishop Stephen Sykes, in an essay entitled "The Incarnation as the Foundation of the Church" in *Incarnation and Myth*, writes,

> To be an Anglican means to belong to a church in which the story of the incarnation is repeatedly rehearsed and implied, in its liturgies, including its most recent revised service books … and in its Canon Law.[12]

We believe then that we are placed by God in a world of variety and diversity. God expects us to work within this complexity, not to hope to escape from it by excluding from that world whatever does not fit our narrow plan.

Some Anglican theologians have described the church as "the extension of the Incarnation." This description is another way of expressing the words of Jesus as recorded in John's gospel: "As the Father has sent me, so I am sending you." We believe that God calls the church into being in order to do God's work. The church is called to transform culture, to make the world a place where God may be known and God's purpose fulfilled. So

---

12 Stephen Sykes, "The Incarnation as the Foundation of the Church," *Incarnation and Myth* (London: SCM Press, 1979), p. 119.

the church cannot avoid being involved in the world, in the needs and issues of contemporary society, in political and social action. Some people may say that the church should not be involved in political and social issues, but in saying so they are denying Anglican tradition and understanding. God calls us to be a message of hope to the world, accepting all its diversity and ambiguity, and working to transform it, to bring the world to its true centre.

The Anglican family

We belong to a family of churches that share a common history, common patterns of worship and forms of government. This is the Anglican Communion — thirty-eight provinces worldwide. Even with this common background, we recognize that there are great differences among family members. We come from many races and cultures. We bring different assumptions and emphases to our discussions when we meet. Yet when we meet, we find that our common membership in the body of Christ is more important than the differences that divide us. In most families there are the eccentric aunts, the brothers who can never discuss politics without a major argument, the children whose decisions challenge the values of their parents. But all are part of the family, and are loved and welcomed because of, or in spite of, their idiosyncrasies. So in the church, the bonds of family are strong and can help us to be more tolerant and understanding of differences. Getting to know each other, keeping the dialogue going, and listening to one another without prejudging or cutting off debate will be essential for Anglicans in this century.

Accepting complexity

It is interesting to note that the discussion around Anglican identity and diversity has parallels with our own national story. In Canada, we spend a good deal of time looking at questions of national identity. How do we, as citizens of a bilingual multicultural country, define our identity? How do we affirm unity while celebrating regional diversity? In *Reflections of a Siamese Twin*, John Ralston Saul says that Canada is *defined* by its diversity: "While all countries are complex, the central characteristic of the Canadian state is its complexity."[13] Canada, he says, does not fit easily with the old monolithic models of other nation states, nor the new monolithic international economic models.[14]

> What might be called Canada's moments of failure can usually be traced to those periods when we feel ourselves … too insecure, too weak, too tired to carry the

---

13 John Ralston Saul, *Reflections of a Siamese Twin: Canada at the End of the Twentieth Century* (Toronto: Penguin Books, 1997), p. 3.
14 *Ibid.*, p. 10.

burden of an essentially complex nature. Then anglophones begin preaching unhyphenated Canadianism and francophones claim singularity as the key to survival.[15]

The parallels with the Anglican Church seem significant. Complexity is our defining characteristic. But, when we become anxious and insecure, we become too tired to "carry the burden of an essentially complex nature" and try to force conformity.

John Ralston Saul says, "For Canadians ... the acceptance of complexity has meant the acceptance of a perpetually incomplete experiment."[16] This, he says, is in contrast to the monolithic structures of nations such as England and France and the United States. He also says, "We are descended from and have been dominated by countries which incarnate the completed experiment.... In the shadow of such powerful 'normalcy' it isn't surprising that we tend to mistake our strengths for our weaknesses."[17]

In the church too this incompleteness causes us anxiety. And in the shadow of other churches whose more monolithic structures suggest completion and certainty, we can be blinded perhaps to the strengths of our "perpetually incomplete experiment."

In May 1999 the Primate of the Anglican Church of Canada, Archbishop Michael Peers, gave an address at Renison College,

---

15 *Ibid.*, p. 10.
16 *Ibid.*, p. 13.
17 *Ibid.*, p. 15

Waterloo, Ontario, on the theme "Challenges Facing the Anglican Communion at the End of the Twentieth Century." In that address, he makes a helpful point about the unity we seek. Unity, he says, "is not about everyone being of the same mind on every issue. Unity is about holding together things that are very different." In Christ, he says, "differences are not made to disappear. Differences are welcomed and honoured and held together. From the vantage point of the kingdom of God, differences give life; they are not a threat to it, nor are they a threat to unity. Our diversity, as much as our unity, gives glory to God."

All of our struggles to define doctrine and authority need to be seen in the wider context of the mission of the church. We are called not to live for ourselves alone but to carry into the world God's message of love for all. That world is a place of diversity and ambiguity. It is a strange land where people's lives are broken and fragmented. But it is the place where we are called by God to live and work. We can offer the world a message of hope, based on our belief that God created the world and sustains it in being; that God sent Jesus to be born into our world and to take on the sufferings of the world, triumphing over evil by his death and resurrection; that God is present and active in our world through the power of the Holy Spirit.

God calls us to work for justice and peace for all, to help others become the people God created them to be. We recognize that there is no single way to experience God in our lives. There are many different kinds of religious experience. Evangelism is action as well as words. People see our faith reflected in the way we behave. Our actions tell them about the real beliefs that govern our lives. We do not know how we influence others. Often a word or action that we may no longer remember turns out to have profoundly influenced someone else. A lifestyle based on the gospel is the best witness to the truth of the Christian faith. The Lord's song then is an action song — a song of deeds as well as words.

CHAPTER FOUR

Looking to the Future in Worship

In the discussion of the tensions that face us as we reflect on Anglican diversity, worship may be considered first because it is the primary reason we meet with other Christians. We come together to give thanks to God for all God's many gifts to us; in the words of the General Thanksgiving,

> for our creation, preservation and all the blessings of this life: But above all for thine inestimable love In the redemption of the world by our Lord Jesus Christ; For the means of grace and for the hope of glory (*Book of Common Prayer*, page 15).

We gather to pray for our own needs and the needs of the world. We are nourished by the Word of God, fed by the sacrament, strengthened by God's Spirit, and sent to carry out our ministry in the world.

Anglicans have a particular relationship with liturgy, which distinguishes us from other churches. The Anglican Church is not a confessional church. We are not able to point to a "confession of faith" that sets out and defines what we believe. Nor do we have a papacy that declares official doctrine.

In the sixteenth century, a number of "Articles of Religion" were drawn up as position statements on certain teachings, made as acceptable as possible to catholics and different kinds of reformers in that turbulent period. There were varying numbers of articles, from six to forty-two at different times, and they changed in their emphasis. Eventually thirty-nine were approved in 1571, and from 1662 they were bound up with the Prayer Book. They are documents of a particular period, addressing the theological controversies of the time. In general, their language is influenced by Lutheranism and Calvinism, though some Anglicans felt that the articles did not go far enough in the direction of reform. Even their most ardent defenders would not claim that they provide anything like a comprehensive statement defining the Anglican understanding of the faith. Indeed, the 1888 Lambeth Conference went so far as to say that the newer missionary churches of the Anglican family should not feel obliged to accept the articles in their entirety. So while some Anglicans have held these up as an important standard — my own confirmation instruction in 1956 consisted of the rector reading aloud the Thirty-Nine Articles to my sister and me — they do not constitute a confession.

Anglican have found that, when we try to define the "essentials" of the faith too closely, we often run into problems. Usually we can agree on the major outline of the faith as set out in the historic creeds, but even the creeds generate controversy when attempts are made to gloss them with particular interpretations. Perhaps one of the reasons the Essentials movement in Canada has stirred up such discussion is that setting out a list of essential beliefs has never been part of the Anglican way of defining doctrine.

The Anglican Church has traditionally expressed its beliefs in the words of the liturgy and in the rubrics that define its practice. What we believe about baptism is found in the words of the baptismal liturgy. What we believe about the eucharist is found in the texts of the liturgy. The rubric specifying that the elements are to be reverently consumed and not merely put back in the sacristy cupboard suggests that the elements of bread and wine are somehow changed in the eucharistic rite. And liturgy shapes our belief. The regular recitation of the Apostles' and Nicene Creeds, the large amount of scripture found both in the readings and the prayers, not only express but also shape our beliefs.

Aidan Kavanagh, in writing about liturgy, has said that "the liturgical act . . . is in fact the primary and foundational theological act."[18]

The liturgical act is in fact the primary place at which the church does theology. The rest is commentary. The British writer A. G. Hebert, writing in *Liturgy and Society* in 1935, said, "The church building and the liturgical acts performed there express something about Christianity which the preacher's words can never give."[19]

Any change to the liturgy necessarily expresses the doctrines of the church in new or different words and forms. Consequently we recognize the important implications of liturgical change,

---

18 Quoted in Louis Weil, "The Gospel in Anglicanism" in *The Study of Anglicanism*, edited by Stephen Sykes and John Booty (London: SPCK/Fortress, 1988), p. 63.
19 A. G. Hebert, *Liturgy and Society* (London: Faber and Faber, 1961), p. 41.

and embark on it slowly and with deliberation. In the nine-teenth century there were continual requests in Canada for revision of the 1662 Prayer Book. But there were great battles between high and low church factions, and between those who wished to add additional services and prayers that would make the book more useful in the Canadian context and those who wished to preserve the Elizabethan compromise and the beauty of the traditional language. Three years after the Canadian revision of 1918, Archbishop Matheson complained:

> I presume you are aware that some of our very advanced men have so far completely ignored the existence of the revised book, and have not even made experimental use of it temporarily.[20]

Almost as soon as this revision was in print, there was growing pressure for further change, and experimentation with liturgical texts took place in many parishes. General Synod of 1943 set a new revision in motion, culminating in the preparation of the book that was given final approval only in 1962.

By then the worldwide liturgical movement was bringing new ideas and emphases to the discussion on liturgical revision. So trial liturgies in contemporary language, produced in booklets of various colours, proliferated. In another twenty years, more or less, the 1985 *Book of Alternative Services* (*BAS*) was

---

20 William R. Blott, *Blessing and Glory and Thanksgiving* (Toronto: Anglican Book Centre, 1998), p. 61.

authorized for use after much testing and discussion. And the coming decades will, I believe, see this process continue.

Critics of the *BAS* argued that a change in the words of the liturgy indicated a change in the doctrine it expressed. More accurately, a change in the words indicates a change in emphasis, bringing to the fore aspects of Christian theology that previously have been understated in our liturgies.

For example, in the *BAS* we find more explicit references to God the Creator and to God's continuing work in creation. Our offering of praise to God the Creator is an important theme of this book. Yet this is not a new idea but an ancient belief.

> I believe in God, the Father Almighty,
> Maker of heaven and earth,
> And of all things visible and invisible.

In the *Book of Common Prayer* we find the Collect for Ash Wednesday, "Almighty and everlasting God, who hatest nothing that thou hast made ... " So the *BAS* is not introducing a new theological position but is reminding us of the fullness of the nature of God.

The eucharistic prayers of the *BAS* represent a broadening of our understanding of the saving work of Christ, identifying that work not simply with Christ's death on the cross but including the events of his life and ministry, resurrection, and ascension. The *Final Report* of the BAS Evaluation Commission describes it thus:

> Salvation is not identified only with forensic acquittal accomplished by the death of Jesus Christ, but more

inclusively with the restoration and renewal of the human position and the creation of the new community.[21]

Again, this is not a new theology but a widening of a strand in traditional theology.

Since the 1950s there have been major changes in our baptismal practice. The 1918 and 1959 Prayer Books encouraged more public baptisms, making baptism part of the regular worship of the community. The directions linked baptism to the offices of Morning or Evening Prayer rather than the eucharist, but in practice, baptism was often celebrated as a private family Sunday afternoon rite. The new rites in the *BAS* stress the place of the worshipping community in welcoming the newly baptized, emphasize proper preparation of parents and sponsors, and draw out the meaning of the baptismal covenant in questions addressed to all the baptized. The new rites emphasize baptism as the full sacramental initiation into membership in the church. This understanding has enabled us to accept children as full members of the church, with the right to participate fully in the eucharist, the family meal. What remains is the perennial question of what to do about confirmation.

Preparing new liturgies requires attention to the diversity of Anglican belief and practice. And any liturgy is apt to emphasize some more than others — just as the old liturgies did. Any book that the Canadian church produces must try to provide

---

21 Book of Alternative Services Evaluation Commission, *Final Report to the General Syod of the Anglican Church of Canada June, 1995* (Toronto: Anglican Book Centre, 1995), p. 60.

forms of service that will be useful standards for the majority of parish churches.

In his delightful little history of liturgy, *1662 and All That*, Dewi Morgan wrote, "Christian worship is not a set of mechanical formulae ... It is a lively relationship with the living God. And, because it is lively, it grows. It is something which grows in the individual life as one grows in grace and perception. It is something which grows in history."[22] The liturgy is not static but always becoming in response to the ongoing activity of God in our lives.

As we look to the future, what might we expect in terms of Anglican worship?

Future liturgical change

Let me first say the obvious: liturgical change is inevitable. Indeed, the words and patterns of Anglican liturgy have been changing and evolving since they came from the pen of Thomas Cranmer. Three prayer books in ten years, setting forth very different doctrinal emphases — this is surely a record, set between 1549 and 1559, a record that we have not wished to match since.

None of our liturgical forms was intended to be fixed forever. Cranmer's preface to the first Prayer Book in 1549 makes

---

22 Dewi Morgan, *1662 and All That* (London: A. R. Mowbray, 1961), p. 27.

it clear that liturgical texts may be revised in order that the liturgy may serve its true purpose — to sing our song of praise and thanksgiving to God. In the liturgy we learn the story of salvation, and we express and celebrate that faith before we go out to bring its good news into our everyday lives.

Anglicans place a strong emphasis on the doctrine of the Incarnation, the belief that, in Jesus, God chose to become human and to share our life. God meets us in our own time and place and in our own culture, not in the culture of first-century Palestine or in the culture of sixteenth-century England. The intention of Anglican liturgy has always been to use the language of the people so that the good news might be understood in our daily life. Liturgy is rooted in our contemporary context.

The Anglican Church of Canada, along with all the other provinces of the communion, has produced new prayer books and other liturgical expressions that use the language of our own people to speak to our own situation. We owe much to the church in sixteenth-century England, but times change. We no longer want to pray in the litany, "From the tyranny of the bishop of Rome, and all his detestable enormities, Good Lord, deliver us." Indeed, some Anglican parishes include in their public prayers "John Paul, the Bishop of Rome" along with a prayer for "George, Archbishop of Canterbury."

It would make no sense in Canada to pray that God will "endue the Lords of the Council, and all the Nobility, with grace, wisdom and understanding" or "that it has pleased thee to appease the seditious tumults which have lately been raised up among us," a reference in the English Prayer Book of 1662 to the recent civil war.

These are interesting historical curiosities when we come across them, but they do not speak to us today about the gospel and our lives. We need, and have produced, our own prayer books that fit the Canadian context. The Christian liturgy must express the gospel to a particular culture, in a particular time and place. The American liturgist Louis Weil has commented on this in a chapter in *The Study of Anglicanism*.

> The need for change is itself an indication that the context in which Christians are living their lives has changed, and with that, that our understanding of our relation to God has shifted to a new ground. Worship is an articulation of faith. Liturgical change is thus an indication of underlying change both in the Church's self-understanding and of the way it understands the God who is the focus of its worship.[23]

The church is not a museum. It is a living organism rooted in particular times and places. We cannot recreate a past age, for the past is as much a creature of our imagination as it is of historical fact. The Christian faith needs to be expressed anew to each new generation of Christians, building always on the foundations of Scripture and Tradition, but expressing and interpreting these in ways that can be understood by contemporaries. Our liturgies continue to be enriched by those of other churches. A changing and developing liturgy is one of the means by which the gospel is communicated today.

23 Weil, "Gospel in Anglicanism," p. 56.

Change takes time. Liturgical change needs a long period of trial and experimentation before words and phrases become approved texts. In Canada, we have approached such change responsibly and well, and I believe that we will continue to work at liturgical renewal in many ways. Ongoing questions of liturgical revision raise concerns: Should we continue to have two liturgical books, or merge them into one? Should we revise the current books or come up with something different? How can we incorporate new ideas and concerns while preserving the best of our tradition? The future will likely be full of liturgical change, considered within the guidelines of Scripture and Tradition and under the customary authority of bishops and synods.

Inclusive language

Anglican worship will continue to move in the direction of greater inclusivity. The rise of feminism in the 1960s and 1970s has brought many changes to the church — the increased participation of women in the government of the church, the admission of women to the ordained ministry, the expansion of the role of lay women in ministry. Feminism has brought a new hermeneutic by which to explore the scriptures and has offered a critique of traditional patriarchal models of authority and government.

None of these contributions has been as controversial as the movement to make our language more inclusive of women. The controversy arises because of the enormous power of language not only to describe our experience but also to shape it.

Language changes us — that is why it is so important and so threatening.

For centuries, a convention in the English language has been to allow the masculine noun and pronoun to represent both men and women. So the *BCP* speaks of "all sorts and conditions of men" and "dearly beloved brethren" in referring to all humankind. Our new liturgies in the *BAS* and the *Book of Occasional Celebrations* have tried to be inclusive in speaking of human beings, using terms such as "all people," "dear friends in Christ," "brothers and sisters."

"What a fuss about nothing!" some have said. "Surely we all know that 'men' includes women too." But the fact is that the old convention has broken down. Our laws are couched in more inclusive terms. When we see the word *Men* on a door, we don't think that the washroom is for women too. In everyday Canadian culture we don't make elaborate translations, such as that "brother" means "sister and brother." We should no longer have to make those translations in our worship. The theological principle that men and women are created equal and in the image of God requires inclusive language. Common courtesy demands it. Although some people may not be offended by sexist or racist language, others are, and it is courteous and just to acknowledge their legitimate concerns.

Do we change the words of the liturgy because some Christians find them excluding, or do we change the words in order to raise people's awareness of the underlying issues? The answer, in good Anglican fashion, is both. We want to speak to the deep concerns of many women and men but we also recognize the power of language to change both ourselves and our culture.

Language, when understood in a new way, creates new understanding. Once you hear language in a new way, you cannot go back to the old. Inclusive language, then, is here to stay, and future liturgical revision certainly will incorporate the principle of inclusivity. Future texts may also recognize the need to be inclusive of children, inclusive of all ages of people, of all races and cultures. I have always loved William Bright's great hymn "And now, O Father, mindful of the love," but I had not noticed anything odd about it until I was singing the hymn with a great many African bishops. When we got to the third verse, we all sang very heartily, "From tainting mischief, keep them white and clear," and I wondered what sort of mental gymnastics they needed to go through in order to make sense of the hymn's implied equation of whiteness and goodness. Happily the words were changed to "keep them pure and clear" in both the red *Hymn Book* and the new *Common Praise*.

In Canada, inclusive language has been the rule for some years, and while there are still occasional grumbles, the debate has cooled. But another and more difficult discussion likely will continue. That is the move to include in liturgical texts a wider range of images when we speak of God, including images that are feminine, such as Sophia or Wisdom, and Mother. These are biblical images, and scholars have helped us to discover the rich treasury of names and images for God that the scriptures contain — the mother hen, the woman seeking a lost coin, the midwife, the mother. Many of these images are used by Jesus himself as he speaks of God's loving relationship with the creation.

Some languages have gender-neutral pronouns. When the scriptures have been translated into certain Asian languages, translators have been able to use gender-neutral pronouns to refer to God as personal but as neither masculine or feminine. However, we must struggle with the limitations of our language.

Any name for God and any description of God is only partial. God cannot be confined by the boxes of any human language. To speak of God as Father — or indeed as Mother — is to express something about the nature of God and God's relationship to the created world, but the name is not everything that we would want to say. Let us put aside our fear and open our minds to a new and deeper understanding of who God is.

Three authorities are available to guide our quest for images to describe the living God. Scripture is the primary source. Tradition offers us both masculine images, such as Lord and Father, and feminine images. Julian of Norwich wrote, "God chose to be our mother in all things," and Anselm of Canterbury wrote, "Jesus, as a mother you gather your people to you; you are as gentle with us as a mother with her children." The third authority, Reason, is an invitation to use our God-given intelligence to delight in the exploration of who God is.

We cannot explore all these issues in depth here, but I believe that they will continue to engage the minds and imaginations of Christians in the future.

Greater participation

Worship will continue to be more inclusive of the whole people of God. The participation of the laity in liturgical ministry has been a major change of the last forty years. It has not been long since the priest did everything — read the lessons, preached the sermon, celebrated the eucharist, and distributed both the bread and the wine. (In some small parishes, he even played the organ!) We now have many people moving in and out of the sanctuary, serving, reading, praying, preaching, administering the bread and wine. And most of the time, they share in the conduct of worship in the ordinary clothes of lay people, thus linking worship with everyday life.

Worship is also becoming more inclusive of children and young people as we recognize and celebrate the gifts they bring. By contrast, not long ago in a congregation there were three teenagers (including our own two) who were keen drama students and regular church attenders, and not once were they invited to use their skills in reading a lesson. Their gifts, while praised and encouraged by the parish, were not seen as having any connection with ministry inside or outside the church . This custom is now changing as young people are involved in a variety of ministries in both the congregation and the wider community.

The Anglican Consultative Council, in the report of its 1996 meeting in Panama, says, "Lay people who are acknowledged as leaders of the larger community, whether in business, education, government, or wherever, should be encouraged to take responsibility in Church assemblies and encounters as well."[24] It continues, "What is experienced and taught within the preaching of the word and the celebration of the Sacraments, both Baptism and Eucharist, must enable the people of God to 'Go, tell, do' — to fulfil their mission to a broken world."[25]

---

24 *Being Anglican in the Third Millenium* (Harrisburg: Morehouse, 1997), p. 150.
25 *Ibid.*, p. 150.

We in Canada have made great strides in this direction. Those of us who have travelled to other provinces of the Anglican Communion realize that we now take much for granted. At the Lambeth Conference of 1988, many bishops were scandalized that lay people were allowed to administer the bread at communion. Their tradition reserved that administration to priests. The assumption still exists in many Anglican provinces that lay people are primarily the recipients of the ministry of the clergy. The coming decades will see, I am sure, a much greater role for lay people, young and old, in the conduct of worship.

The needs of teenagers and young adults are a particular concern. Their questioning of the faith and exploration of the self need encouragement and understanding. We have to ask, What is it that makes the church seem less relevant to this age group? How can we make the church a place of welcome and inclusion for them, a place where we take seriously their questions and concerns? A first step may be simply to listen to their concerns and to invite them into a conversation about their lives and the Christian faith.

Hearing each other's stories is an important part of making the church a welcoming and inclusive place. It is harder to exclude people once you know them as persons and have heard a little bit of their story. Telling our individual stories is new to Anglicans, who traditionally have tried to practise a polite reserve. But I believe our church is being enriched by this increased sharing. It is also helping us to deal with some of the issues that divide us — from ecumenism (where Anglicans and members of other denominations or faith traditions can come to understand each other's faith and experience) to issues of human sexuality (where we can meet others with different beliefs and lifestyles and see how their personal stories connect them to the story of the Christian family). The Episcopalian author Howard Hanchey says that evangelism is less a ministry of talking than it is a ministry of listening — hearing others tell their story and helping them to identify the places in that story where God has touched their lives.

As an old maxim says, one Christian is no Christian. None of us is able to live the Christian life in isolation from other members of the body of Christ. Being a Christian means being part of a larger community, a community whose members we may not otherwise have chosen to associate with. Painful as we may find it, we are in the enterprise together with people of different views, emphases, and beliefs. We cannot force uniformity on this community. The attempt would only lead to fragmentation. Jesus calls us to live as members of one body, struggling to work out what that means.

Worship as evangelism

Worship in the future must be seen as part of our evangelism. In most cases it is the worshipping life of the congregation that attracts others to join us. In books such as *They Became Anglicans* by Dewi Morgan and *Modern Canterbury Pilgrims*, edited by James Pike, many of those who chose the Anglican Church wrote that they did so because of Anglican worship. I know that this was so in my own life, as I moved from the Roman Catholic Church of my childhood to the joys of Anglican worship and a small church choir. Coming from pre-Vatican II Rome, I thought that the *Book of Common Prayer* was almost contemporary in language!

The worship of God is our primary calling, and it should be offered in such a way that God is praised and others are inspired to join. Worship, well done, takes time and energy to prepare and carry out. Something so central to our Christian life deserves our very best, and the great attention that we Anglicans pay to worship is none too much. Archbishop William Temple, in a BBC broadcast in 1944, said, "The world will be saved from political chaos and collapse by one thing only: that is worship."[26]

As an educator, I believe that education is the key to everything that we do in the church. Whether or not we do it intentionally, we are educating others by everything we say and do. If our greeting is cool, we are teaching people that their presence in our community is unimportant. If we ride roughshod over the opinions of others at a parish council meeting and do not give people a chance to express differing views, we are saying, "My opinions are the ones that count." If we never visit the homes of our fellow parishioners, we are likely to be understood as thinking that we are too busy and too important to visit. If we are ill-prepared for worship and sloppy in conducting the service, we are suggesting that worship really is not important.

---

26 Donald E. Messer, *Contemporary Images of Christian Ministry* (Nashville: Abingdon Press, 1989), p. 107.

Clergy and laity today must learn to be what British liturgist Michael Perham calls "liturgically bilingual." Since we have moved to Ottawa, we have discovered a new appreciation of the importance of French/English bilingualism. Clerks in stores, receptionists in offices, flip with ease from one language to the other, and we are envious of their skill. We recently spent a year at the University of the South in Sewanee, Tennessee. At this theological college, seminarians who wanted to minister effectively in the south were learning to conduct the liturgy and preach in Spanish.

Liturgical bilingualism means developing understanding and fluency in both our liturgical books — understanding and loving the *Book of Common Prayer*, which has shaped our church and contains texts that help us define who Anglicans are, while understanding and loving newer texts such as the *Book of Alternative Services*, which attempt to be faithful in presenting the Anglican tradition to our contemporary Canadian society. Jesus speaks of the householder who brings out of his treasure what is new and what is old (Matthew 13:52). We too have liturgical treasures new and old.

The traditional services connect us with the communion of saints, with all those generations who have worshipped in our churches before us. Yet there are many Anglicans who have never used the *BCP* and for whom the *BAS* is the old tradition. Oddly enough, they may be upset by new experimental services and regard them as a departure from the old familiar words of the green book. I became an Anglican in 1956, and so was not dismayed by the changes that we made when we started to use the revised *BCP* in 1959. It quickly became for me the old familiar liturgy.

Common prayer

Liturgy in the next few decades will continue to develop and change as the Christian community strives in each new era to be faithful to God. As a church, we help people to bring their everyday lives to God so that these lives may be transformed and empowered by God's grace. In worship, God transforms the meaning of things (bread and wine, water, oil) in order to transform us. Our worship rises out of the community and its concerns, and builds and strengthens that community for its mission in the world.

The Anglican Church is built on the principle of common prayer. Our worship follows a particular pattern as set out in authorized books. Customs may vary from time to time and from place to place, but the basic forms remain the same. To outsiders, these set texts may seem limiting or even boring. To Anglicans, they provide the freedom to relax into the familiar texts and explore them week by week. The texts are crafted in such a way as to allow us to reflect on the themes of the gospel in a regular sequence. They include both penitence and praise. Yet within these forms there is room to express the particular concerns of this time and place. The common text frees us from dependence on the personality or special interests of the minister. Even the spontaneous worship of some liturgical traditions quickly becomes ritualized, following the same pattern week by week. Public liturgy by its very nature is not spontaneous. It is the common work of the people of God, and not that of individuals.

Part of the tension of our Anglican identity is expressed in the way we make decisions about liturgy. In our episcopal form of government, the bishop is the chief liturgical authority within the diocese. Synods may draft and recommend experimental liturgical texts, but only the bishop can authorize them for use in a particular diocese. In the case of the *BAS*, permission was given to publish for use "where permitted by the diocesan bishop." This is a strength (allowing the trial use of new rites) and a caution (placing some controls on experimentation).

An interesting example is the case of a eucharistic prayer prepared by writers of *The Whole People of God*, the popular ecumenical curriculum developed by Wood Lake Books and widely used in Anglican parishes. Anglicans pointed out, I think to the surprise of United Church members of the writing team, that such a service could not automatically be used in Anglican churches without authorization. The Doctrine and Worship Committee of the Anglican Church and a number of bishops and others looked at the text and decided that it did not contain all that Anglicans would want to say in a eucharistic prayer. So a number of bishops declined to authorize the prayer for use and suggested instead texts from the *BAS*. We have diversity in liturgy, but we have agreed that it should be authorized diversity.

The *BAS* evaluation commission recommended to General Synod that supplementary material be prepared, including a eucharistic rite that is inclusive in its language and imagery about God, a eucharistic rite that embodies a Reformed theological understanding of the eucharist, and rites that would allow aboriginal communities to incorporate cultural and spiritual traditions. In this way we continue to develop new liturgical texts within our system of authority.

In 1967 a commission was set up in the U.S. Episcopal Church to advise the presiding bishop on the controversy arising from some of the statements of Bishop Pike of San Francisco. The report wanted to encourage theological speculation and inquiry, but then went on to say,

> We do believe that if an individual finds himself unable, in good conscience, to identify with the living tradition of the church, reflected in the Bible, the creeds, and, especially for Anglicans, in the liturgy of the Book of Common Prayer, he should as a matter of personal integrity voluntarily remove himself from any position in which he might be taken to be an official spokesman for the whole community.[27]

This commission made it clear that identification with the common prayer of the church is a part of the living tradition that we hold as Anglicans.

Let me close this chapter with some words from the American liturgist, Louis Weil, in *The Study of Anglicanism.*

> Liturgical rites are not ceremonial clothing for doctrinal teaching. Rather than *teaching* the faith, in the usual sense of that word, the liturgy *celebrates* the faith. It lifts it up through words and signs in a corporate experience

---

27 John Macquarrie, "The Anglican Theological Tradition" in *The Anglican Tradition*, edited by Richard Holloway (Toronto: Anglican Book Centre, 1984), p. 33.

which expresses the faith which has summoned the people to gather. Yet it also nourishes that faith, and sends the people forth to live it in their daily lives. It is a transforming experience in which the people themselves are renewed as a sign of the mystery which they have assembled to celebrate.[28]

The liturgy, he says, connects with our current lives, but it also points ahead to God's future action. Thus it will continue to change and develop under the guidance of the Holy Spirit as both sign and promise of God's work of redemption. The church is rooted in a particular time and place, yet God's purposes are always unfolding. So the liturgy will continue to change and develop as it celebrates our faith in God in each generation.

---

28 Weil, "Gospel in Anglicanism," p. 56.

CHAPTER FIVE

Looking to the Future in Ministry

Ministry in the last forty years has changed dramatically. Within this brief space of time, significant events have altered forever the way ministry is understood and carried out.

Anyone who has been ordained for forty years can think back to the time when they were theological students, and the very different kind of church in which they were preparing to be employed. Theological students were all male, mostly first-career people, fresh out of university, in their early to mid-twenties. They were single and lived in residence, able to share in all the worship and social life of the community. They were preparing themselves for full-time positions in parishes. They expected that they would be the "parson" or "person" in the parish — the one who would take services, visit parishioners, preach and teach, run parish meetings — in short, do it all. They expected to be appointed to the care of souls by the bishop without perhaps even having visited the parish. Certainly the appointment did not need any assent from the local congregation. We have come a very long way in the last forty years for reasons both theological and sociological.

The first of these reasons is our renewed understanding of the meaning of baptism. By our baptism, we become members of the body of Christ incorporated into the family of the church. The baptismal covenant spells out our responsibilities. We are called to a life of service to others, of evangelism, of action for justice and peace. As lay people come to understand their membership in the church in terms of active participation in its mission and ministry, so this participation has expanded not only to assisting in the conduct of worship such as in the prayers and the readings, but also to sharing in the ministry of outreach, education, and pastoral care. Lay people do this not because they wish to compete with the clergy, but because it is their right and responsibility as part of the community of the baptized.

The second factor is the development of a good deal of thinking about the laity, the people of God. In 1958 Hendrick Kraemer wrote *A Theology of the Laity*, a book that marked a significant change in the way the church understood ministry. Volumes have since been written about the ministry of lay people, both within the worshipping community and in their daily life and work. Writers such as Verna Dozier (*The Authority of the Laity*) and William Diehl (*The Monday Connection*) and many others have helped us to expand our vision of the laity as the people of God.

Today we find in the church a "better educated" laity — people who read theology and are not afraid to ask theological questions or explore theological concepts. Lay people are no longer content to leave theology to the clergy. They are no longer content to be simply the recipients of the teaching of the clergy, but are actively taking charge of their own learning. The "small group" movement of the 1960s began a process by which learners were encouraged to take an active part in their own learning. Fredrica Thompsett's book *We Are Theologians,* is an encouragement to us all, clergy and lay, to see ourselves as theologians, involved in the exploration of the Christian faith.

The third factor, one of enormous significance in the life of the church, has been the opening of ordained ministry to women. It is now so much a part of our life in the Anglican Church of Canada that it is hard for us to remember how recently this came about. I was a theological student in the early 1960s, a time when very few women studied theology. There were three of us in a class of eighteen, and most other classes had even fewer women students. We embarked upon this path because of a love of learning and an interest in exploring theology. We did well academically — at my college women traditionally led the class in academic standing — but we certainly had little prospect of employment in the church or even much share in its government.

At that time, there seemed to be very little discussion about the ordination of women. I recall a conversation with Archbishop Howard Clark, perhaps around 1966 or 1967, in which he spoke of a place for women as lay theologians of the church but not as ordained clergy. Yet how quickly all this changed in Canada. In 1969 Archbishop Clark, in response to the request of General Synod, set up the Primate's Task Force to study the question of the ordination of women.

In 1971 the House of Bishops authorized the ordination of women to the diaconate, and recognized that those women who had been formally "set apart" as deaconesses were within the order of deacon. In 1973 General Synod voted in all three orders to accept the principle of the Ordination of Women to the priesthood, though it was not until 1976, when the legislation had proceeded through the proper channels and had been approved at the 1975 General Synod, that the first women priests were ordained. This was a mere eleven years after my graduation from theological college, when such a possibility had not even been raised. Indeed, evidence that this was not seen as a live possibility is found in the fact that women were exempt from certain classes in pastoral theology — how to celebrate the eucharist, how to baptize, how to choose hymns. There was clearly no possibility that we would ever need these skills.

Since that time many Canadian women have been ordained, including two women to the episcopate, and the church has been enormously enriched by their ministry. Though there were differences of opinion — often severe — on the ordination question, these differences have largely been resolved over the years. While there may yet be individual resistance to the ordination of women, the mood in general throughout the Canadian church is one of acceptance. All dioceses of the Anglican Church of Canada now have ordained women among the clergy. All bishops now accept the ministry of ordained women. When we hear of the continuing struggles to promote the ordination of women in other parts of the Anglican Communion, we Canadians are surprised and wonder what the fuss is all about. In twenty-four years our decision has become fully incorporated into the life of our church. And it is hard to remember how earth-shattering, how foundation-shaking, that decision was.

The decision to ordain women is perhaps a good model for us to look at as we consider how to deal with diversity in the Anglican Church. This was indeed as divisive as any issue could be.

The conflict was rooted in doctrinal difference. What does priesthood mean? In what sense does the priest "represent" Christ at the altar? Are women by their nature less capable of certain roles than men? How do we interpret the Bible when it says that women must keep silent in church? When it says that the man is the "head" of the woman? When it says that in Christ there is neither male nor female?

Such a decision challenged centuries of tradition and custom. Though there is some evidence that women played a larger role in the leadership of the early church than we have acknowledged — perhaps were even ordained leaders in the very early period — the overpowering weight of tradition in the church has justified an all-male priesthood.

Making decisions

How did we in Canada come to make such a significant change in church tradition? We were second only to the Anglican diocese of Hong Kong as we boldly went where few Anglicans had gone before. Reflecting on the decision making process might be helpful in our understanding of how we maintain Anglican identity in the midst of a diversity of theological positions.

Three elements stand out.

1. The first is a willingness to prepare for the discussion and to let the process take its own time to unfold. Many of the issues that come before the church are complex. Taking time to

research and study the background to these issues is time well spent. It is easy to make snap judgements without taking time to explore an issue in its complexity. So papers need to be written, expert opinion sought and weighed, discussion undertaken as widely as possible among church members. All this needs to be communicated and shared openly. Even though some issues may be painful and difficult, the whole church needs time to engage in the discussion. One strength of Anglicanism, at its best, is its willingness to explore complex and difficult issues, not prejudging too soon, yet not being swayed prematurely.

2. The second element, an important preparation for discussion about how much diversity the Anglican Communion can bear, is a need to look closely at Holy Scripture and see how it informs our decision. This is not as simple as declaring, "the Bible says." The Bible says many things; some verses contradict other verses. The Bible is not a simple book. It is complex, diverse, nuanced. An interesting book called *The Bible Tells Me So* by Jim Hill and Rand Cheadle sets out on facing pages the scripture verses that support and oppose a particular point of view — a useful reminder that interpreting and understanding the Bible is far from simple.

It is not helpful to turn debates on major theological issues into games of biblical ping pong, hurling texts at each other. We must look behind the biblical texts and try to articulate for ourselves and others what makes us choose this passage in support of our argument and reject another passage that might undercut our point of view. Why, for example, do we discount Jesus' clear teaching against divorce and remarriage and yet accept at face value other verses that appear to condemn homosexuality? We are selective in our interpretation of scripture, and one of the things that distinguishes one Christian church from another is the way each interprets scripture. This study of interpretation, known to scholars as *hermeneutics*, is far removed from a quick and easy jotting down of proof texts.

3. The third element in making decisions in a time of diversity is a willingness to stay connected with the wider communion and to remain faithful to the ways of decision making that we have agreed to follow both nationally and internationally. The Anglican Church has developed a process of synodical government in which decisions governing the life and teaching of the church are made by bishops, clergy, and laity meeting together. We may not always agree with the results, but we have agreed to follow this model of making decisions.

On the international level, provinces of the Anglican Communion have agreed to meet to discuss issues. While it is not required that all provinces move together on an issue, nevertheless agreements are made giving permission for provinces to act and committing other provinces to respect those decisions. In other words, one province will not break off communion with another once permission has been given.

Take, for example, the question of the ordination of women. The ordination issue was on the agenda of the Lambeth Conference of 1968, and the conference affirmed that the theological arguments for and against the ordination of women were inconclusive, and thus there was no clear theological objection to such ordination. The bishops asked every province of the communion to study the question. In 1971 the Anglican Consultative Council, with representative bishops, clergy, and lay people from every province, advised the bishop of Hong Kong and any other bishop acting with the approval of his province that "if he desires to ordain women to the priesthood, his action will be acceptable to this Council; and that this Council will use its good offices to encourage all provinces of the Anglican Communion to continue in communion with these dioceses." These statements were not mandatory, forcing a uniformity of practice on the church, but were permissive, allowing a province to make a decision according to its own canons, and agreeing that all provinces would respect this decision.

This model of permitting and respecting diversity, I believe, will stand us in good stead as we meet each new challenge.

Only chaos will result from abandoning our agreed-upon ways of making decisions. Using again the example of the ordination of women, we can note the difference between the Canadian and American churches in accepting this decision. In Canada, the Anglican Church moved slowly through the process of synodical decision, taking at least five years to go through all the required steps. In the United States, a few bishops and women candidates anticipated the decision of the General Convention, and an irregular ordination took place several years before regular ordinations were authorized. While I believe that the American church is more deeply polarized on a number of issues including the role of women in the church, I also believe that actions that bypass the traditional canons and decision making procedures of the church can only deepen these divisions. One of the elements that holds our church together is agreement on a form of government. If we wish to change this government, there are ways to do so. Diversity must exist in tension with agreed structures.

Our changing society

In addition to these major theological factors in the development of our understanding of ministry, sociological factors have caused us to rethink our traditional understanding of ministry. Rural depopulation for country parishes means smaller numbers of active church people to maintain church buildings and programs, smaller numbers to pay the stipends of seminary-trained professional clergy. The money is no longer there. Smaller numbers have pushed rural communities into multipoint groupings with other congregations in order to share the cost of providing priestly ministry in the area. Ecumenical working arrangements with other Christians in the community makes sense in some situations, yet in other places, it has been difficult to overcome our reluctance to give up our own church building, to change our cherished traditions of worship. The problem of providing ministry in sparsely populated areas manifested itself first in areas such as the prairies or the British Columbia interior but is now beginning to be felt in other parts of Canada. Similar concerns exist in urban areas with changing populations.

For all these reasons, ministry needs to be planned and carried out in ways different from those we have relied on in the past. I believe that we are at the beginning of a period of great variety in forms of ministry, a period of experimentation and evaluation, as we try to discern how we can be the church in our own situation.

What are the reasons behind the need for new forms of ministry? Society is increasingly secular, multicultural, and multifaith. The common cultural base derived from Christianity has disappeared. The church has lost its privileged position, assumed authority, and influence as commentator on events and values. People are too busy with competing activities, time-tables, demands, and pressures to have time for religion. Both rural and urban economies are changing, and with them the distribution of population. There is stiff competition for charitable funds, which places financial restrictions on church programs. At the same time, there is pressure on the church and other voluntary organizations to pick up the slack for social services that are no longer publicly funded. Less money is available to pay full-time professionally trained stipendiary clergy, but more and more social and political issues of great complexity demand a reasoned and faithful response from the church. Furthermore, clergy are called upon to minister in situations of diversity and change, and need training and support in these new times. Happily an increasingly well-educated laity is ready to be challenged to take up their baptismal ministry.

Ministry needs to be embodied in a variety of ways in this period of social change. Some of the new forms of ministry likely will prove to be of lasting value and will be incorporated into the life of the church in a formal way. Some may prove on evaluation to have limited use and will be only a footnote to the history of ministry in our time. But I foresee a continuing period of exploration and assessment. This diversity will bring — has already brought — great blessings, but it has also brought great tension as we look at new ways of doing ministry in contemporary society.

We need to be guided by those enduring touchstones of Anglican theology discussed in chapter 3:

Scripture: Is what we are doing in ministry consistent with our understanding of the person and work of Jesus Christ? Do our patterns of ministry help us to proclaim the good news of God in Jesus Christ to our contemporary society?

Tradition: Are our new patterns of ministry consistent with our Anglican understanding of order and authority? Do they combine the wisdom of the past with an understanding of tradition as dynamic and developing?

Reason: Are these new patterns based on our best knowledge about ourselves and our Canadian society? Are we using the best resources, the best strategies of planning and evaluation?

Theological education

One of the keys to developing new forms of ministry lies in new models of theological education. The question, How might ministry be done in new ways? requires the further question, How can we best prepare people for ministry in these changing times? What gifts and skills are necessary for ordained and lay leaders in the church today? And for seminaries the question is, How can we become resources for, and partners in, that training?

Already we are seeing a variety of different ways in which theological training is delivered. Preparing aboriginal leaders for priesthood in their own native communities requires different methods and delivery of training than preparing stipendiary clergy for city parishes or training local ministry teams for pastoral responsibilities in rural congregations. Theological education increasingly needs to be varied and flexible. Bishops and ministry committees and theological educators are already looking seriously at these questions as they respond to the needs of the church for persons trained for a variety of ministries.

Let me give you my dream of what theological education might look like in a renewed Anglican Church.

In my dream, I would like to see the parish once again became the setting for serious and lively theological education. Until the mediaeval period, the parish was the location of theological study. Lay students gathered with the clerks in holy orders to study the scriptures and the teachings of the church. But gradually the locus of theological education shifted to the religious orders and then to the seminaries, and this study became the special preserve of the clergy. Imagine what it would be like if the basic elements of theological education were available to all lay people in parishes. These parishes would become lively centres of learning and debate, with clergy and lay people working together as partners in learning. Lay people would be strengthened in their own faith and ministry as they deepened their understanding of scripture, church history, and doctrine. They would feel that their capabilities, skills, and hunger for learning were being taken seriously by the church.

In my dream, all people in the parish would have the opportunity to develop a basic understanding of the Christian faith within the cultural setting in which they live. Those who feel a call to a particular ministry, ordained or not, could then go on to further specialized preparation for that ministry. The seminaries could take up the work of preparing people for particular ministries, knowing that these people were already grounded in the basic teachings of the Christian faith. And all the time that the seminaries currently spend laying the ground-work for the exploration of the faith could be spent in deepening this understanding and helping people to learn the skills of par-ish and other ministries.

I dream of a church where people come together to share their stories and to bring the events of their lives into dialogue with the story of the Christian faith. This church would be a distinct and valued community in the midst of an impersonal culture, a place where each person's story is heard and prized by others. I dream of a church that knows the story of God's peo-ple, that retells and celebrates this story in public worship, and grafts all its members into this story through baptism and the eucharist.

I dream that theological education will help people to use today's movies and novels and plays and poetry to understand the spirit of our age. It will help us to understand the changes occurring in the world and prepare the church to deal with them. A church so prepared will be continually renewing, and renewed by, its expression of the faith.

Is it realistic to expect that lay people can be involved to this extent? Let me tell you a story about our daughter Becky. When she was five, she attended a special children's hour on Good Friday while the traditional service was going on in church. The teacher was a young woman who did not regularly teach the children. She read to them three different biblical accounts of the crucifixion and talked a little bit about the dif-ferences in them. Becky came bounding into the parish hall after the service, full of excitement. "Dad, Dad! Did you know that Mark says this about Jesus being crucified? And Matthew says something different." She had no difficulty at the age of five in understanding the very basic principle of biblical criticism, that different authors tell different versions of events. If she could understand and be excited by this idea at the age of five, it suggests to me that we are sometimes short-changing the people in the pews.

I believe that people in the church hunger for learning about the Christian faith and want to incorporate this learning into everyday life. And I hope and pray that the next decade in the church will be one of a renewed emphasis on teaching and learning. Seminaries should be a place where parish clergy will develop the skills in education and training to carry out this ministry. It will be important for clergy not just to retain and share large chunks of information, but to learn to think theologically — to bring the events of everyday life into dialogue with the scriptures and the tradition of the church, and then to help lay people to learn to think theologically about their everyday life and work. The job of the teacher is not to tell people *what* to think but to help them discover *how* to think. Clergy will need to be well trained in educational methods, group dynamics, and leadership skills, as well as in the content of theology.

Clergy must see themselves as partners in ministry with lay people. The rite of ordination of a priest makes this clear: "You are to nourish Christ's people from the riches of his grace, and strengthen them to glorify God in this life and in the life to come." At a consecration, the bishop elect is asked, "Will you encourage and support all baptized people in their gifts and ministries, nourish them from the riches of God's grace, pray for them without ceasing, and celebrate with them the sacraments of our redemption?" The clergy as partners in ministry are there to nourish and support all the people of God in their life and ministry.

I dream of a church where lay people come together to worship God, to learn about the faith, to receive the sacraments, to share with other Christians in exploring what it means to be the body of Christ at this time in this community. I dream of a church where each member shares, as appropriate, in worship and learning, in outreach and service, each offering their gifts of knowledge and skill for the building up of the body of Christ and for the spreading of the good news of God's love for all humankind. The parish as the place of worship and learning, the seminary to help us all develop the skills to do this — these are my dreams for this new century.

CHAPTER SIX

Social and Ethical Issues

In our contemporary society we are faced with many ethical issues of great complexity. New technology allows doctors to prolong life, to perform challenging and expensive surgical procedures, to attempt untried strategies for reproduction. Other issues such as capital punishment, gambling, and care for the environment present church members with difficult decisions.

Along with many denominations, the Anglican Church of Canada has been struggling for some time with issues of sexuality in general and homosexuality in particular. The Anglican Church includes many gay and lesbian Christians, both clergy and laity. The church has studied the subject since the mid-1970s and has provided excellent material to help Anglicans reflect on the issues involved. Anglican views on homosexuality and homosexual relationships probably reflect the whole gamut of opinion on this controversial topic.

How do Anglicans deal with their diversity on divisive issues? The challenge is to maintain certain fundamental principles while acknowledging a diversity of Christian opinion.

One factor informing Anglican moral statements has been the recognition that theological statements can seldom be absolute — can seldom be either black or white. Most theological issues are so rich in complexity that the language used about them must be nuanced and balanced to express this complexity. It is possible to see a Christian viewpoint on both sides of many moral issues facing the church. Sometimes we crave the certainty of absolute pronouncements — this is absolutely right, that is absolutely wrong. Yet I think, if we are honest, we must acknowledge that ethical issues seldom present themselves to us as clear-cut. And very often these issues wear a human face, which makes our absolute stand, our support or condemnation, more difficult.

It is easy to condemn the idea of young people living together before marriage until your own young people do it. It is easy to condemn the remarriage of divorced persons until it happens in your own family. It is easy to condemn homosexuality until you meet faithful homosexual Christians living in committed relationships. Every absolute is challenged by circumstances, and no position on any issue can be enforced without working though the implications in the lives of Christians.

Anglicans recognize that Christian doctrine is dynamic and open to interpretation and exploration in the light of Scripture and Tradition under the scrutiny of Reason. We place a high value on scholarship and study. We have an approach to our faith that allows us to ask, Does this make sense? This reasoned approach equips us well to look at today's complex issues.

Another factor informing Anglican moral statements is the way of decision making that Anglicans have developed over the years. We look to the whole church to help us make decisions. Our faith is not just a matter of private individual decisions.

Historically, and even today to a lesser extent, bishops have a good deal of power to make decisions independently of others. But as a church we have agreed upon a synodical form of government in which clergy and representative lay people share with the bishops in making decisions that affect the life of the church. So we have increased variety of opinion on any issue. If we commit ourselves to this principle of synodical government and trust to the guidance of the Holy Spirit, then we commit ourselves to abide by the results. Rather than leaving to found our own church when the majority decision goes against our wishes, we are committed to working within the structures we have set up, making decisions together, working for change from within these structures.

Sometimes the church changes its mind. The 1920 Lambeth Conference spoke clearly against the use of artificial means of birth control. By 1930 the bishops had come to a different point of view. While still stressing the importance of family life and parenthood as the "foremost duty" for married people, their report stated, "We cannot condemn the use of scientific methods to prevent conception, which are thoughtfully and conscientiously adopted." We try to work together under the guidance of the Holy Spirit to reach a common mind.

In our approach to canon law, Anglicans have tried to uphold the same principle of fewer rigid definitions. In 1987 a set of "Pastoral Guidelines for Interchurch Marriages" was agreed upon by Canadian Anglicans and Roman Catholics. The introduction to these guidelines helps us to understand the different approaches to law in the two denominations. In Roman Catholic canon law, the laws are strictly stated and are to be interpreted "with all the personal adaptations contained ..." In other words, there is the possibility of a number of exceptions to the law. Anglican canon law is based on English common law. The laws are few, but they are to be strictly interpreted. Our practice is to define very little, except for the affirmation of certain fundamental principles.

When Anglicans make decisions, often these are expressed in permissive rather than obligatory terms. The principle of admitting baptized children to the eucharist is affirmed. Parishes may institute this practice within certain guidelines (asking the permission of the parish council, obtaining the agreement of the parents and children), but no parish is *compelled* to institute it.

This principle is particularly true of decisions made by the provinces of the Anglican Communion. The structures that allow members of the worldwide family of Anglican churches to meet together have no legislative authority over the autonomous provinces. The Anglican Consultative Council, the Lambeth Conference of bishops, the Primates' Meetings, can suggest and advise but cannot compel. Recognizing that there may be significant differences of opinion among Anglicans, the councils give permission to some provinces to act on certain issues. For example, permission was given for the ordination of women and for admission of baptized children to the eucharist before confirmation. It was not that this permission was needed before a province could act, but it was an acknowledgement that each province is a member of a larger family, and it expressed a willingness to consult before asking. A province may proceed upon a course of action but no other province is compelled to do so.

Principles of decision making

In summary then, here are what I see as the principles of making decisions in a time of diversity.

We need to recognize that making decisions on complex issues takes time. It takes many years for the church to study and debate divisive issues. Our impatience for action needs to be tempered by a willingness to take the time to allow a large number of Anglicans to form an opinion. Synodical decision making takes years, especially if it involves canonical change. A more monolithic structure like the Roman Catholic Church can decide to adopt a vernacular liturgy, and the change can take place in a relatively short time. For Anglicans the authorizing of contemporary liturgical texts takes much longer.

We need to hear and respect different views, acknowledging that Scripture and Tradition may be quoted to support each side of the argument. The Anglican historian Fredrica Harris Thompsett describes Anglicanism as a conversation.

> I like envisioning Anglicanism as "a conversation" with "different voices speaking for scripture, for tradition, for reason, and for experience." This rings true to my assessment of the sixteenth-century church of the English Reformation, as well as the Episcopal Church today. It is helpful to envision Anglicanism as a dialogue that searches faithfully for comprehensive understanding.[29]

---

29 Fredrica Harris Thompsett, *Living with History* (Cambridge: Cowley Publications, 1999), p. 175.

We need to look always to our touchstones of Scripture, Tradition, and Reason, and to our own experience, being open to the guidance of the Holy Spirit who teaches us new truths in every age.

We need to see if there is a larger principle that can illuminate conflicting views, or views that are incomplete. This larger principle can allow us to live with both views in the light of this greater truth. We need to seek the broadest understanding on which we can agree, rather than asking every Anglican to dot each *i* and cross each *t*. As the Lambeth Conference of 1968 urged,

> Comprehensiveness implies a willingness to allow liberty of interpretation, with a certain slowness in arresting or restraining exploratory thinking.[30]

We can continue to make decisions that are permissive, not mandatory, as the consultative bodies of the Anglican Communion do. This will allow some Anglicans to act on decisions while not requiring all Anglicans to do so. Of sacramental confession, Anglicans have said, "All may, none must, some should." These words can be guides also for the kind of permissive decision making we recommend.

We can accept the uneasiness of our present situation, recognizing that this is a time of profound change, and not being too quick to force uniformity on a church that has never been uniform in its practice. We can learn to value ambiguity for the

---

30 *The Lambeth Conference 1968 Resolutions and Reports* (London: SPCK, 1968), p. 140.

elbow room it gives us. Perhaps we can return in our language to the poetic, the nuanced, the imaginative, to give us words patient of several interpretations in which to vest our statements.

Above all, we can accept with joy and thanksgiving our membership in a community. Belonging to a family brings with it lots of stresses. A family is a group of different people, with different personality traits, different annoying and endearing habits, yet joined together by deep bonds of affection, of shared experience, of family history and tradition. None of us could survive without the support and care of others, either our birth family or a family we have chosen. We are created to live in community. So in the church we must remember that we are in this together, as part of one family. Learning how to live together is a challenge — but it is the only way.

CHAPTER SEVEN

Living with People of Other Denominations and Faiths

Ecumenism

As Christians, we live in a multidenominational society. As Canadians, we have always been aware of other churches. In a country in which over 45 per cent of the Christians are Roman Catholics, it is hard not to be aware that we live side by side with Christians of other traditions. But for most of our history it has been easy for us to live together with other Christians in our neighbourhood, at our jobs, at our schools, and yet to live separate lives on Sunday. We have worshipped with others of our own ethnic background, our own language, our own customs. On the prairies, we were known as the "English church." Germans, Ukrainians, and Norwegians had their own churches. And though we might meet at the post office or on the curling rink, we did not meet in church.

As our society becomes increasingly secular, as the Christian community shrinks, Christian denominations will need to work more closely together. Part of the impetus may come from declining membership and resources. We can share ministry in sparsely populated areas. We can continue to finance mission and ministry by pooling our resources of money and personnel.

But the major impetus must come from the gospel imperative — from Jesus' words, "That they all may be one." We are called by God to work for the unity, redemption, and reconciliation of the whole human race, because all people are created and loved by God. The church is called to be a sign of unity and hope to the world.

From earliest times the Christian church has been divided by differences of belief and practice. Centuries of history — old differences, old resentments and persecutions — divide us. These divisions weaken our witness to the world. Yet in the twentieth century we saw a remarkable movement to draw together the churches in greater understanding and agreement. The Edinburgh Missionary Conference in 1910, the World Conference on Faith and Order at Lausanne in 1927, the formation of the World Council of Churches in 1948, the Canadian Council of Churches, the ecumenical coalitions (a particularly Canadian approach to social action) — all these ecumenical organizations allow the participating churches to share ideas and resources, and to express some common understandings in the world context and in the local situation.

Bilateral discussions between ourselves and other partner churches help us to understand differences of belief and practice, and to come to agreements on faith and practice where this is possible. An example is the Anglican-Roman Catholic International Commission, which has published several statements worked on by members of both denominations. A document such as *Baptism, Eucharist and Ministry* from the World Council of Churches represents a remarkable agreement in those areas. In Canada and the United States, Anglicans and Lutherans have lived side by side for a century but have not always known each other well, as each church in the early days represented a particular ethnic heritage. Anglican-Lutheran dialogues at the national and international levels have allowed the two churches to move towards recognition of members and ministry, eucharistic sharing, and greater cooperation.

The challenges of ecumenism in the twenty-first century are similar to the challenge of defining Anglican identity. How much unity can be maintained in diversity? Are those things we hold in common sufficient to overcome our differences of belief and custom? Sometimes it is ecumenical dialogue that helps Anglicans to focus on the larger principles — on what is central to the Christian faith — and to recognize as less important personal denominational and cultural practices. Ecumenism can help to teach us how to live faithfully in the midst of diversity.

Anglicanism has maintained the threefold order of ministry — the ministry of bishops, priests, and deacons — even though our interpretation of the role and authority of the three orders in the ministry of the whole church has developed and changed. Ecumenical dialogue, particularly with churches with a single order of ordained ministry, has forced us to examine more closely our understanding of ministry. This was true in the 1940s when the churches of the Indian subcontinent participated in discussions that led eventually to the formation of the united churches of South India, North India, Pakistan, and

Bangladesh. This was true also of our conversations with the United Church of Canada in the 1960s and 1970s. It is true today in the working out of agreements between the Anglican Church of Canada and the Evangelical Lutheran Church in Canada. All of these discussions have been complex and difficult. They have forced members of all denominations to look at their understanding of church and ministry.

We rejoice that Anglicans and Lutherans have come to an agreement that allows for a recognition of each other's ministry. This agreement has come about because the two churches have been able to look at the larger principle — the gospel imperative to unity — in order to witness to God's work of bringing wholeness to a broken world, and to allow that principle to take precedence over other principles for the good of the church and the world. This dialogue has not been without its tensions: both Lutherans and Anglicans have had to look at the role of bishops, of priests and pastors, and of deacons, and to examine the theological principles of oversight and proclamation and service that are being expressed in ordination. We give thanks that these discussions are coming to their fruition.

I see in ecumenism a model for living with diversity. It is a model that takes a long time, that encourages openness and dialogue, that depends upon a will to struggle to discern the truth. It is a model that returns to the basics of the faith — to scripture, to the historic creeds and the teachings of the church. The American New Testament scholar William Countryman has attributed the differences among denominations to the different ways in which each interprets scripture. Each denomination is like a different set of lenses by which we view the biblical record. So any dialogue among churches must begin with a rigorous examination not only of the words of scripture but also of the hermeneutic or principle by which we interpret scripture.

Anglicans have long been committed to ecumenical dialogue. This model of exploration and dialogue that includes openness to different views and a willingness to test these views against the gospel imperative for unity is a helpful model for dealing with diversity within our own church.

Today Anglican parishes work with neighbouring congregations in a variety of ways — sharing facilities, running joint programs, studying and worshipping together from time to time. Local grassroots ecumenism is essential — getting to know each other is a first step to closer ties.

Ecumenical activity, the cooperation among Christians of different denominations, is widespread throughout the life of the church but is not always recognized as such. Most congregations are in fact already ecumenical in that many parishioners have come to the Anglican Church from other Christian denominations. They have married Anglicans. They have moved to a neighbourhood where it is convenient to attend an Anglican church. The local Anglican church has good music or a good youth group. There are many reasons, both theological and secular, that bring people to our church. They bring with them their heritage in worship and teaching, and still no doubt have a network of friends and connections within their former church family. In the workplace, in voluntary organizations, Anglicans work together with other Christians and find a commonality that allows them to work together for shared goals.

Congregations themselves are able to tolerate a variety of theological emphases, which allows members to worship and work together while continuing to explore doctrinal differences. We don't expect all members of a parish to have exactly the same understanding of Christian doctrine before we allow them to worship with us. We permit a certain flexibility of understanding in order to allow the Christian community to carry out its ministry and mission in a particular place. This tolerance can be a good model for Anglican unity in diversity in the larger settings of dioceses and provinces, and in the Anglican Communion as a whole.

Interfaith dialogue

As well as living in a multidenominational country, we live in a multicultural and multifaith country and world. As early as the 1970s, Canadian ecumenists were heard to comment that there were more Muslims in Canada than there were Presbyterians. This number is significantly higher today. A trip on a Toronto bus or a visit to a shopping centre is enough to convince us of this. Even on the prairies — once home to aboriginal Canadians and European immigrants — our society is becoming increasingly multiracial and multicultural. Here too we face the question of diversity and the church's witness in a racially and culturally mixed society.

Life was sharply different in the nineteenth century. We behaved differently. We went to another country, we brought people there the gospel and the benefits of our European civilization, we converted them from their own religions and planted the church firmly in their land. We expected everyone else to stay where they were. Since then two changes have occurred.

The first is that people from those other lands are here now, living and working beside us. Sometimes they look just like us. Sometimes they look different, and their religious differences are obvious by their dress and customs. We cannot ignore the fact that Canada now includes people with different beliefs. Organizations such as the Royal Canadian Legion and groups such as the Royal Canadian Mounted Police have had to find ways of being inclusive to Sikh members for whom the wearing of the turban is a religious custom.

The second difference is that Christians have begun to enter into dialogue with people of other faiths. Rather than simply trying to convert them to Christianity, we have begun to approach them in a spirit of understanding and acceptance. Sometimes we have been drawn to this dialogue by a need to work together to deal with injustice and discrimination. Sometimes we have been drawn by a deep desire to understand and appreciate the way God works in human lives. Sometimes our children marry their children and the impulse for dialogue and understanding is focused in the family.

There are theological principles that move us to interfaith dialogue. We believe that there is one God who has created the world and all humankind. There cannot be "their God" and "our God." There is one God whose revelation we have received in a particular way, but who (we believe) is large enough to be worshipped in other ways. So a desire to learn more about the one God leads us into dialogue with others who believe that they too know something of God's revelation.

But what are we to do with the words of Jesus? Words like,

Go into all the world and preach the gospel to the whole creation (*Mark 16:15*).

Unless you eat of the flesh of the Son of Man and drink his blood, you have no life in you (*John 6:53*).

No one comes to the Father except through me (*John 14:6*).

Can we balance these with other words?

In my Father's house are many rooms (*John 14:2*).

I have other sheep that do not belong to this fold (*John 10:16*).

Living with diversity demands that we struggle to understand and interpret scriptures that are far from clear or one-sided.

How do we strike a balance between acceptance of other faith traditions and tolerance for a diversity of religious belief, and yet remain a faithful witness to the uniqueness of Jesus Christ? These questions will continue to challenge us as we try to define our Christian identity in an increasingly multicultural and multifaith Canada. Dialogue and openness are imperative if we are to be faithful to the God who created all people in the world and who loves and sustains that creation. Again, this dialogue among diverse positions strongly held will demand our best efforts as we work under the guidance of the Holy

Spirit, with the revelation we have received in Scripture and Tradition. Simply writing off other religions as outside our concern will be neither possible nor indeed honest. God has created a world of human diversity and we need to figure out what this means.

We are involved in this interfaith dialogue not only as individual parishes and denominations but also as worldwide churches. So Anglicans and Lutherans must continually explore what it means to be part of a world communion. We are part of a family of churches that includes people of many races, cultures, languages. We are brothers and sisters of Anglicans whose life experience is very different — of Anglicans who in the Sudan and Malaysia are living under Muslim rule, of Anglicans who are Palestinian in Israel, of Anglicans in Northern Ireland whose Protestant history and links with England place them in conflict with Roman Catholics. We have family history and family loyalties, and we need to support and understand Anglicans who live in persecution and conflict. Yet we live in Canada, and so we must also try to discern what the gospel means here in our own country where the conflicts of other countries do not need to be fought. Interfaith dialogue is another way in which we as a church are stretched to understand and live with increased diversity.

Both ecumenism and interfaith dialogue require that we learn more about our own faith in order to express this faith to others. When we enter into dialogue with people whose beliefs are different from our own, we must look more closely at our own beliefs, and learn to articulate and express them in ways that others can understand. If the church is to survive and be strong, we must learn more about the Christian faith and about the church in which we are members. One of the great gifts of interchurch and interfaith dialogue is the strengthening of our own faith.

CHAPTER EIGHT

Authority in the Anglican Communion

All our discussion about the future of the Anglican Communion rests upon our Anglican understanding of the nature of authority. Who speaks on behalf of Anglicans? What is the authority behind those statements? How do we make decisions when there seem to be conflicting authorities?

The report of the Lambeth Conference 1948 describes authority in this way:

> Authority, as inherited by the Anglican Communion from the undivided Church of the early centuries of the Christian era, is single in that it is derived from a single Divine source, and reflects within itself the richness and historicity of the divine Revelation, the authority of the eternal Father, the incarnate Son, and the life-giving Spirit. [31]

---

31 *The Lambeth Conference 1948* (London: SPCK, 1948), p. 85.

Dispersed authority

The report goes on to say that authority is found through six sources: Scripture, Tradition, the Creeds, the Ministry of the Word and Sacraments, the witness of the saints, and the "consensus fidelium" (that is, the continuing experience of the Holy Spirit through the lives of faithful people in the church). Holy Scripture is a basic authority for Christians because it is the record of God's revelation to human beings. The Tradition of the church and the historic creeds also have authority because they represent the church's faithful working out of the meaning of God's revelation down through the centuries. Authority is exercised in the local community through leaders called by God and the church to a ministry of proclamation of the Word, administration of the sacraments, and service to others. In the Anglican Church, this authority is exercised through the threefold ministry of bishops, priests, and deacons, formally chosen and lawfully ordained, and through synodical government in which lay people share with the clergy in decision making. Authority must be received continually and accepted by the church under the guidance of the Holy Spirit, a guidance that is given to the church in all times and places.

The Lambeth Conference1948 report goes on to say that authority "is thus a dispersed rather than a centralized authority having many elements which combine, interact with, and check each other."[32] And herein lies much of our difficulty as

---

32 *Ibid.*, p.86.

we as Anglicans try to steer our way through the maze of "authorities" that are intended to be complementary but can sometimes seem competitive. We find ourselves caught between the example of denominations with a strong central authority, whether that be a single interpretation of scripture or a centralized form of government, and the post-modern philosophy that questions and distrusts all authority.

We have in the past had certain ways of defining authority. The *Book of Common Prayer*, for example, has defined the standard of Anglican worship. The ordination oaths require the use of the *Book of Common Prayer* "and no other except ..." The latter phrase allows for the use of contemporary liturgical texts when authorized. At one time, Anglicans all over the world used versions of the 1662 *Book of Common Prayer*. Now the liturgy is found in many languages and in many new forms.

The threefold ministry of bishops, priests, and deacons has an authority that links the local with the universal church, and the contemporary church with the church throughout Christian history.

We recognize the authority of Scripture, interpreted by Reason and scholarship in the light of Tradition. Yet at the Lambeth Conference of 1998 some bishops expressed concern that the Anglican Communion was being pushed by some bishops in the direction of a more literal interpretation of the Bible. This prompted the Anglican Association of Biblical Scholars at their annual meeting in October 1999 to make a response. (For the full text of their response, please see the appendix, page 124.)

We are concerned by claims to understand Scripture univocally, especially with regard to urgent moral, political and ecclesiastical questions where the community of the faithful has not reached a consensus. Such claims often minimize the complexity of Scripture, short-circuit the hard work of prayerful discernment, and polarize the community of the faithful along lines of "right" and "wrong" interpretation.

The biblical scholars go on to quote the Archbishop of Canterbury, George Carey, speaking on issues of homosexual persons in the church:

> Argument and controversy solve nothing. We need a new kind of "conversation" — one that begins with respect for the integrity of another and a willingness to study the scriptures together; to reflect on our experience — including the experience of homosexuals; and to share a process which attempts to put into practice "the Church as a community of moral discourse."

We need to devote much more time to developing an understanding of the authority of scripture that respects the complexity both of scripture and of the issues that confront us, and that includes a wide range of scholarly interpretation as part of the conversation.

Structures of authority

A uthority might be described as rightful power, or the power to act to cause things to happen. How then do things happen in the Anglican Church? At the local level, the bishop consults with clergy and laity to make decisions affecting the life of the church in that area. The bishop has a good deal of power to make decisions alone; yet these decisions, in order to be incorporated into the life of the community, must have fairly widespread assent. So authority is exercised by bishop, clergy, and laity consulting together. Synodical government — the bishop acting in diocesan synod — is an important way in which authority is expressed for Anglicans.

At the national level, authority is expressed by structures upon which we have agreed — by General Synod and its councils and committees that represent us. The authority lies in our agreement to decide matters in this way. Worldwide, we have agreed-upon structures that provide for us "centres of authority" — the office of the Archbishop of Canterbury, the Lambeth Conference, the Primates' Meeting, and the Anglican Consultative Council.

The role of the Archbishop of Canterbury has historical significance for member churches of the Anglican Communion. The Archbishop of Canterbury is a diocesan bishop and the Primate of All England, but he also serves as president of the Lambeth Conference and of the Anglican Consultative Council, calling dioceses and provinces together to confer. The Report of Lambeth 1968 called this "a primacy of honour, not of jurisdiction." Though the archbishop does not have direct authority over Anglicans in the way that the Bishop of Rome has over members of the Roman Catholic Church, the office serves as a focus for unity in the communion.

The Lambeth Conference, held every ten years, is a conference in which every diocese of the Anglican Communion is represented. An invitation to attend the conference is, in fact, a test of being part of the Anglican Communion. For several years in the mid-1980s, there were two archbishops in the Sudan, each with bishops and clergy loyal to him. The dispute was finally settled only when one archbishop received the Archbishop of Canterbury's invitation to attend the 1988 Lambeth Conference.

The Primates' Meeting is a more recent addition to the consultative process, providing an opportunity for bishops who are heads of provinces to confer together. The Anglican Consultative Council, an international group of about seventy-five people, began meeting in 1971. It provides an opportunity to include representative clergy and lay people along with bishops in discussions on matters of faith and practice.

All these structures are consultative rather than legislative. Their reports and resolutions cannot compel obedience, but they can and do speak with a moral authority that is respected. On many potentially divisive issues — the use of artificial means of contraception, the ordination of women, the admission of children to Holy Communion before confirmation — the statements of all these groups have provided permission for parts of the communion to move forward while still maintaining communion with other Anglican provinces.

Stephen Sykes writes, "The distribution of God's gifts to the whole Church means that there are voices of authority, not one unequivocal *voice* of authority." Sykes goes on to say, "These voices of authority are the consequence of the call of God to every Christian believer to embody the saving Gospel in his or her own life, and to receive the empowering gift of his Holy Spirit to that end."[33]

Authority comes as a call of God and a gift of the Holy Spirit. Individual Christians receive the authority proper to sons and daughters of God in their baptism, and are challenged to live it out in faithful obedience to God's will. The church as community participates in the power of Christ and of the Holy Spirit. This power is shared in the church by clergy and laity — by clergy chosen and ordained for the ministry of word and sacrament, and by lay people who hear and respond to the word of God and who share in the life and government of the church. All authority stems from the spirit of Christ who fills the church and leads it into truth. And Christian authority is found in individuals and institutions when the spirit of Christ is discerned in them.

Future discussions

Where might our current discussions on the nature of authority take us in the future? Anglicans have affirmed an understanding of authority that is dynamic and changing.

---

33 Stephen Sykes, *Unashamed Anglicanism* (New York: Seabury Press, 1978), p. 169.

Historically we have upheld certain principles — episcopal government defined as the bishop acting in synod, common prayer using authorized liturgical texts, the participation of the laity with the clergy in decision making — while allowing some freedom of interpretation and some permission to develop forms and structures suited to particular places. Historically our methods of consultation have been permissive rather than legislative, rejecting uniformity and unilateral decisions. It would not be true to the best in Anglicanism to compel obedience to a narrow set of principles.

We need to maintain communication among all parts of the Anglican Communion by encouraging gatherings such as the Lambeth Conferences and the Anglican Consultative Council (ACC). It is expensive to hold such gatherings, but it would be much more costly in terms of understanding and insight if we no longer met face to face. We need also to keep groups such as the ACC representative of laity and clergy as well as bishops. Some have suggested that the Primates' Meeting might replace the ACC. Since we believe that authority is not found exclusively in the episcopate but is more widely dispersed in the church, the body of Christ, it is important that the fullness of the church's membership be represented in any discussion of the life of the church.

Being in communion with the See and Archbishop of Canterbury is a visible sign of membership in the Anglican Communion. Recently some have asked whether the president/primate of the Anglican Communion need always be English, or whether the role of president might not be held by a bishop from some other part of the Anglican Communion. Such a decision would let it be seen clearly that the Anglican Communion is not defined by "Englishness" and would reflect the diversity of the Anglican Church and its dispersed authority.

Authority and ecumenism

The question of authority is focused more sharply for us in our dialogues with other Christian denominations. The most recent agreed statement of the Second Anglican Roman Catholic International Commission (ARCIC) is called *The Gift of Authority*. It is the third in a series of agreed statements on authority. This document looks particularly at the teaching authority of the church, at the principle of synodality (how the church consults with its members in making decisions), and at the possibility of a universal primacy exercised by the Bishop of Rome. These are three areas in which our two churches have viewed authority in different ways, and they are not questions that will easily be resolved. Our Anglican tradition has led us much farther in the direction of synodical government than has developed in the Roman Catholic Church. This mutuality is part of the way Anglicans experience and understand authority.

The universal primacy of the Bishop of Rome raises questions for Anglicans because we have not understood primacy in this way. Primacy for us must be exercised collegially and synodically, in consultation with the clergy and laity of the church. A primate exercises leadership in preaching and teaching, yet this teaching needs always to be open to the judgement of Scripture, Tradition, and Reason, and exercised in dialogue with the whole church. The concept of "infallible authority" in one particular location does not reflect the view of the presence of the spirit of Christ, present and active throughout the whole church.

Agreed statements such as these remind us of the different views of authority in different churches. How are such documents "received" and made operative in the life of a denomination? All of the ARCIC statements have followed a similar pattern of reception. They have been forwarded to each province of the Anglican Communion, where they have been studied widely by committees, dioceses, and parishes. In Canada, the General Synod has voted to express the view of the Anglican Church of Canada. The responses from all Anglican provinces have then been forwarded to the Anglican Consultative Council, which has the responsibility for international dialogues with other Christian churches. When practical, a response is also made by the Lambeth Conference. It takes a long time for Anglicans to make a response, because our system of authority is dispersed among the provinces. In contrast, the response of the Roman Catholic Church came after a period of study by the Vatican, without a widespread discussion in dioceses around the world.

Yet even with our differences, we must still commit ourselves to engage deeply with other Christians on questions of the nature and exercise of authority in the church. Distrust of external authority is general in contemporary Western society. There is a strong sense of individual responsibility and of an internal authority validating individual actions. Yet often in such a climate, we may long for an authority to which we can give absolute obedience. We may look for someone to make all our decisions, allowing us to escape from that painful responsibility.

In religion, some are looking for absolute truths in scripture, choosing one single interpretation and ruling out any others. Some look for absolute definitions of essential beliefs, not allowing the questions that arise to be asked for fear of disturbing these definitions. Some look for absolute authority in people who will make firm decisions on a given topic.

But Christianity is not this simple. As we have seen, the scriptures contain words patient of many different interpretations, words that contradict and puzzle. Our definitions of the faith are always incomplete, inadequate to express the full meaning of Christianity. People who are placed in authority must be open to the full range of the meaning of the gospel.

We need to take responsibility for our life of faith. As Anglicans, we have a number of instruments of authority that enable us to live as members of Christ's body, the church. While the several instruments of authority will likely continue to develop, it seems clear that our commitment to the principle of dispersed authority will remain an important part of our life as a communion.

Conclusion: What Is the Future of the Anglican Communion?

For the Martin Lectures, on which this book is based in part, I chose the title "The Compass Rose: Flowering or Fading?" The Compass Rose is the compass surmounted by a mitre and encircled with the words *The Truth Shall Make You Free*. It is the symbol of the Anglican Communion: the points of the compass describe a worldwide family of churches, the mitre shows our common history and pattern of government and authority, and the verse from the New Testament witnesses to the church's faith in the risen Lord Jesus Christ (John 8:32). The symbol is embedded in the floor of Canterbury Cathedral, the mother church of the Anglican Communion, and it is recognized throughout the world as a sign of who we are.

Is this rose flowering or fading? The Anglican Church is famous for its tolerance of diversity. Has this diversity at last been pushed to its limit, perhaps beyond its limit? Many contentious issues are being focused sharply for us by the very different cultures from which Anglicans come.

At the Lambeth Conference in 1988, the strength seemed to lie in the large number of bishops from the Episcopal Church in the United States. Though their church membership is about 2.5 million (more than double that of the Anglican Church of Canada), the number of dioceses (109) is in a much higher proportion than our own thirty dioceses for a million members. The Church of England has only forty-four dioceses for the 26 million members it could claim. So the American church has a large number of dioceses relative to its membership. In 1988, the Americans were a strong presence at Lambeth, and many of their concerns, particularly the role of women and the ordination of women to the episcopate (then not permitted in England), dominated the agenda and the news media.

Ten years later, at the Lambeth Conference of 1998, there was a shift in representation. The church in Africa has grown tremendously in the last ten years and many new dioceses have been created. There are now 221 African dioceses. This creates a significant presence in any world gathering of Anglicans, and it is natural that the concerns of the African bishops are at the centre of any discussion. Many of these dioceses are living with persecution, civil war, refugees, discrimination from governments, the scourge of AIDS and other diseases. They are still deeply involved in the work of primary evangelism, bringing the good news of Jesus Christ to those who are hearing the gospel for the first time. Moreover, there are now ninety bishops from the Asia and Pacific region, including bishops of the united churches, and they too have concerns quite distinct from those of the North American bishops.

The result of this shift in balance is a very different agenda for an international conference of church leaders. The issues of churches in affluent and increasingly secular European and North American societies are of less importance than previously. Many of the African and Asian provinces of the communion hold a conservative evangelical theology and a conservative interpretation of scripture. Many would prefer that issues around homosexuality not even be raised at these international meetings. They sometimes even insist that there is no problem about the treatment of homosexual persons in their countries, though evidence clearly points to the opposite conclusion. When such questions were raised and discussed at Lambeth 1998, tensions were high and debate became acrimonious and hurtful. Does this indicate a split in our family that may be too bitter to heal? How can the communion be held together in the face of such deep divisions?

It is important to affirm that diversity is necessary in order to preserve unity. The Holy Spirit works by presenting us with new challenges and opportunities in each time and place. Insisting on a single rigid interpretation of doctrine is not only contrary to the nature of Anglicanism but it is rejecting an openness to the movement of the Spirit today. We need to continue to learn from each other.

There continue to be challenges and differences of opinion. In February 2000, two priests of the Episcopal Church in the United States were consecrated in Singapore as bishops by the Archbishop of South East Asia and the Archbishop of

Rwanda. They were consecrated as "missionary bishops" to return to the United States to minister to conservative congregations who fear that the Episcopal Church has departed from the traditional doctrines of the church in its decisions on such matters as the ordination of women and the inclusion of homosexuals in the life and ministry of the church.

These consecrations mark a significant departure in the life of the Anglican Communion, when archbishops are consecrating bishops to serve in another autonomous province of the communion. The Anglican Communion has followed the principle of one diocesan bishop with jurisdiction in a particular diocese. Territorial integrity has been a long-standing principle of episcopal order from the early days of the Christian church. As Anglicans, it has not been our practice to adopt overlapping jurisdictions, with a visiting bishop coming in to minister in another's diocese. There have been a couple of exceptions — the parallel convocations of Anglican churches in Europe (one under the jurisdiction of a British bishop and one an American) and the English authorizing of the so-called "flying bishops" who come into a diocese to minister to those opposed to the ordination of women. But these have been exceptions rather than the rule, and perhaps these arrangements will change over time.

The Singapore consecrations, however, represent a new challenge to Anglican structures and a new interpretation of the role and authority of bishops within our system of government. Every Anglican province has canon laws that govern the appointment of bishops for work within that province. The consecration of bishops for work in another province does not follow that canon law. The Archbishop of Canterbury, a few weeks after the consecration, wrote to all Anglican bishops to tell them that he could not recognize the episcopal ministry of the two American priests.

The effect of actions such as these irregular consecrations is to hinder any possibility of dialogue and to close the debate on the important issues that divide Anglicans. As William Countryman says,

> If Anglicanism is to survive as a communion — that is, in maintaining actual communion among its very diverse members across the world — it will do so only by acknowledging the centrality of its spiritual tradition ... In so far as we decline to do so, we shall probably try to substitute, at the heart of Anglicanism, the kind of doctrinal and disciplinary rigidity that we have both rejected and coveted in the Reformed and Roman traditions. If we do so, we will tear Anglicanism, both as a community and as tradition, into increasingly smaller pieces.[34]

Again, I want to affirm strongly that I am hopeful about the future of the Anglican Communion. I have tried to show that our history and our distinctive way of doing theology are ideally suited for helping the church to survive and grow through periods of division and in a world of great diversity. We have done it before, and I believe we will do it again.

---

34 *The Poetic Imagination: An Anglican Spiritual Tradition* (Maryknoll: Orbis Books, 1999), p. 190.

I believe that the communion will continue to survive, as it has in the past, by the goodwill of its members. The bishops of the communion were first called together in 1867, at the invitation of the Archbishop of Canterbury (but at the suggestion of the Canadian bishops) in response to the controversies surrounding the teachings and the authority of Bishop Colenso of Natal. Clearly it was believed that the benefits of face to face conversation outweighed the difficulties of distance and the time and expense of overseas travel. Consultation among bishops has been an important part of our life for a century and a quarter, and in the last three decades the consultation has been expanded to include representative clergy and lay people. There is no substitute for getting to know others personally. Hearing each other's stories helps us to understand the deeply held positions of the other, and makes it harder to condemn outright or to walk away. So I believe that all the members of our communion need to continue to meet, talk, and work together on difficult issues.

The Virginia Report of the Inter-Anglican Theological and Doctrinal Commission, presented to Lambeth 1998, reminds us that

> in addressing issues raised by the complexities of contemporary life, solutions will in some cases be necessarily provisional. There are times when the path ahead is insufficiently clear for categorical claims to be made. Forming a mind entails learning from those within the Anglican Communion and being in partnership and dialogue with ecumenical and interfaith colleagues. There is merit in the Anglican approach of listening to others,

of holding each other in the highest degree of communion possible, with tolerance for deeply held differences of conviction and practice.[35]

We need to maintain the balance of the universal and the particular, allowing local churches to reflect their own situation and culture while affirming the universal principles and teachings of the Christian faith. So our communion may well reflect different practices but still be grounded in the unity of our faith in the triune God.

Konrad Raiser, general secretary of the World Council of Churches, sees diversity not as a sign of disunity but a sign of vitality. Our diversity proceeds from our response to God's call to proclaim the gospel of Jesus Christ in the local context. He writes,

> It is precisely the local concrete obligation arising out of sharing in the history of Jesus Christ, the task to proclaim the gospel of the kingdom of God as a concrete message of liberation and to enable it to take concrete form, which constantly produces fresh differences within and between congregations. These differences are not signs of a lack of unity, but signs of vitality in the body of Christ — provided that they do not erect exclusive

---

35 The Virginia Report of the Inter-Anglican Theological and Doctrinal Commission, in *Being Anglican in the Third Millenium* (Harrisburg: Morehouse, 1997), p. 232.

boundaries between one another or infringe the essential inter-relatedness of the Spirit-produced community.[36]

As Christianity becomes incarnate and rooted in the different cultures of the world, so it will inevitably take on different forms and emphases. There must be a variety in order for there to be unity. Keeping open the dialogue among these various local embodiments of the church is essential.

We need to ensure that any dialogue includes all the theological strands in our Anglican tradition. Conservative evangelicals, liberal catholics, charismatics, middle of the road Anglicans — these and others need to keep listening to each other and not opt out of the discussion.

We need to pursue dialogue on contentious issues, not on the basis of emotion and misinformation but with serious and careful study of Scripture and Tradition. We need particularly to look at the way we use scripture in debate. Why is it that we choose certain passages of scripture to bolster our arguments and yet discount other passages? An honest acceptance of the ambiguity of scripture and of its layers of meaning is perhaps helpful when wrestling with difficult theological issues.

We are sometimes frightened by what we hear bishops and other theologians saying. We need to remember that the writings of individual theologians are part of the ongoing exploration of Christian truth, no more and no less. Their words may encourage us to explore the church's faith and to restate and

---

36 Quoted in William Adam and Graeme Smith, "Hidden Ecumenism: New Priorities for Ecumenical Work," *Theology*, vol. CIII, no. 816: pp. 422–423.

reaffirm it in language for today. So we do not need to be afraid of Anglican thinkers who are exploring beyond the boundaries of our traditional statements of faith; instead, we can affirm their courage in challenging the church to express the gospel faith today.

We need to find ways to learn about and to celebrate diversity. We may learn to understand and appreciate the different views of others, but we may also need to learn to agree to differ. One of the hallmarks of the post-modern age, recent thinkers tell us, is greater diversity and less conformity throughout society. It will be important to affirm that, beneath this diversity, is our deep belief in the good news of the Christian gospel. The Virginia Report sets the challenge of diversity and interdependence in the context of our faith in God the Trinity.

> The Commission . . . believes that the unity of the Anglican Communion derives from the unity given in the triune God, whose inner personal and relational nature is communion. This is our centre. This mystery of God's life calls us to communion in visible form.[37]

After setting out the story of the saving work of Jesus Christ, the Commission goes on to say,

> The Holy Spirit bestows on the community diverse and complementary gifts . . . God the Creator blesses people with many talents and abilities. The Holy Spirit

---

37 *Ibid.*, p. 233.

graces individuals with special gifts. The outworking of one person's gift in the Church is unthinkable apart from all the others. The mutuality and interdependence of each member and each part of the Church is essential for the fulfilment of the Church's mission ...

The variety and difference among Christian charisms would quickly become incoherent and disabling if it were to become eccentric, without a reference to its centre in Christ. An important function of life in communion is always to remain attentive to one another, particularly when conflict arises, so that the centre may never be forgotten. Seen in the framework of God's mission of love in Christ and the Spirit, the variety of gifts, which may appear to be potentially divisive, is seen to be necessary, mutually enriching, and a cause for thanks and praise to God.[38]

This section of the report concludes, "God invites his people to enjoy diversity." I think it is important as we begin a new century that we enjoy the diversity that has been so much a part of our history. We are sometimes grumpy about our differences. A little enjoyment might help us to see these differences in the light of God's call to diversity.

Elizabeth Templeton, a Scottish Presbyterian theologian, encouraged us to enjoy diversity when she described the Anglican Church to the bishops of the 1988 Lambeth Conference.

---

38 *Ibid.*, pp. 240–241.

Both internally and in relation to other evolving Christian life-forms, you have been conspicuously unclassifiable, a kind of ecclesiastical duck-billed platypus, robustly mammal *and* vigourously egg-laying. That, I am sure, is to be celebrated and not deplored.[39]

Michael Ramsey, Archbishop of Canterbury and noted theologian of the church, makes a similar point when he describes the nature of the Anglican Church.

While the Anglican Church is vindicated by its place in history, with a strikingly balanced witness to Gospel and Church and sound learning, its greater vindication lies in its pointing through its own history to something of which it is a fragment. Its credentials are its incompleteness, with the tension and the travail in its soul. It is clumsy and untidy, it baffles neatness and logic. For it is sent not to commend itself as "the best type of Christianity," but by its very brokenness to point to the universal Church wherein all have died.[40]

To be a Christian requires a tolerance for imperfection. The Anglican Church is broken and incomplete, but it points beyond itself to the universal church, the body of Christ. In our

---

39 *The Truth Shall Make You Free*, The Lambeth Conference 1988 (London: Church House Publishing, 1988), p. 292.
40 Michael Ramsey, *The Gospel and the Catholic Church* (Cambridge: Cowley Publications, 1990), p. 220.

brokenness and incompleteness, we are nevertheless strengthened and enabled to minister in a divided church to a world broken and in need of healing.

I believe that the Compass Rose is still flowering, and will continue to flower. I believe that the Anglican Communion will continue to provide a way for Anglican Christians to work together to discover how to communicate the good news of God to all the world. Tensions and divisions challenge us to work with other Anglicans and other Christians at understanding and living the Christian faith. They challenge us to continue to explore how God is calling the church at the beginning of the twenty-first century. Let us work together in a spirit of cooperation, tolerance, generosity, giving others the benefit of the doubt. Of course it is not easy. But it is the only way forward. May God the Holy Spirit continue to guide our exploration.

Appendix

A Response to the 1998 Lambeth Conference of Bishops

Adopted by the Annual Meeting of the Anglican Association of Biblical Scholars,

October 20, 1999.

While Scripture has always been read with profound and prayerful seriousness in the Anglican communion, our tradition has usually been wary of claims to be guided by "Scripture alone." We are aware that faithful persons of good will may reach different conclusions regarding the interpretation of Scripture. Indeed, history has shown that the community of the faithful has sometimes come to discern God's will only after a protracted, agonizing, and contentious process. The struggle against slavery in the 19th century United States is a case in point. In our own day, people of good faith may hold soundly-reasoned, divergent positions of the Bible's significance for questions including the ordination of sexual minorities, the nature of Christian mission, and Christian postures regarding war, international debt and a host of other issues.

We respect the crucial role of conscience in discerning God's will through the enlightening work of the Holy Spirit. We also respect the tremendous complexity of the biblical materials and of the history that produced them.

For those reasons, we are concerned by claims to understand Scripture univocally, especially with regard to urgent moral, political, and ecclesiastical questions where the community of the faithful has not reached a consensus. Such claims often minimize the complexity of Scripture, short-circuit the hard work of prayerful discernment, and polarize the community of the faithful along lines of "right" and "wrong" interpretation.

The understanding of human sexuality is a case in point. The bishops at the 1998 Lambeth Conference acknowledged a variety of "understandings" among themselves relative to Scripture and homosexuality, a point underscored by Presiding Bishop Frank Griswold as well.

We welcome the counsel of Archbishop of Canterbury George Carey, directed to issues of homosexual persons in the Church but appropriate to broader conversations on the role of Scripture in our common life.

"Argument and controversy solve nothing. We need a new kind of 'conversation' — one that begins with respect for the integrity of another and a willingness to study the scriptures together, to reflect on our experience — including the experience of homosexuals — and to share a process which attempts to put into practice . . . 'the Church as a community of moral discourse.'"
We are further confident that a wide range of interpretive perspectives such as those provided by historical criticism, theological-pastoral concerns, feminist/womanist studies, and socio-economic analysis (to name only a few) have a salutary place in such conversations.

We call upon lay and clerical leaders in our Communion to cultivate an atmosphere of abiding mutual respect around the interpretation of Scripture, respect for the complexity of the questions that face us all as we strive to live out our baptismal covenant, and respect for one another as persons who share the enlightening and gracious presence of the Spirit of God.

Bibliography

Adam, William, and Graeme Smith. "Hidden Ecumenism: New Priorities for Ecumenical Work." *Theology*. Vol. CIII, no. 816. November/December 2000: pp. 412–425.

Bateson, Mary Catherine. *Composing a Life*. New York: Atlantic Monthly Press, 1989.

Baycroft, John. *The Anglican Way*. Toronto: Anglican Book Centre, 1980.

Bays, Patricia. *This Anglican Church of Ours*. Winfield: Wood Lake Books, 1995.

———. *Meet the Family*. Winfield: Wood Lake Books, 1996.

Being Anglican in the Third Millenium. Report of ACC X, Panama City. Harrisburg, Morehoues, 1997. Compiled by James M. Rosenthal and Nicola Currie. Harrisburg: Morehouse, 1997.

Believing in the Church: The Corporate Nature of Faith. A report by the Doctrine Commission of the Church of England. Wilton, CN: Morehouse-Barlow Inc., 1982.

Blott, William R. *Blessing and Glory and Thanksgiving: The Growth of a Canadian Liturgy*. Toronto: Anglican Book Centre, 1998.

Book of Alternative Services Evaluation Commission. *Final Report to the General Synod of the Anglican Church of Canada June, 1995*. Toronto: Anglican Book Centre, 1995.

Booty, John. *The Episcopal Church in Crisis*. Cambridge: Cowley Publications, 1988.

Borsch, Frederick Houk. "The Ministry and Authority of Bishops." *Outrage and Hope*. Valley Forge: Trinity Press International, 1996.

Simons, John, ed. *The Challenge of Tradition: Discerning the Future of Anglicanism*. Toronto: Anglican Book Centre, 1997.

Countryman, L. William. *Biblical Authority or Biblical Tyranny? Scripture and the Christian Pilgrimage*. Cambridge: Cowley Publications, 1994.

———. *The Poetic Imagination: An Anglican Spiritual Tradition*. Maryknoll: Orbis Books, 1999.

Diehl, William E. *The Monday Connection: On Being an Authentic Christian in a Weekday World*. New York: Harper Collins, 1993.

Dozier, Verna. *The Authority of the Laity.* Washington: The Alban Institute, 1982.

Evans, G. R. *Authority in the Church: A Challenge for Anglicans.* Norwich: Canterbury Press, 1990.

Fenhagen, James C., with Celia Allison Hahn. *Ministry for a New Time.* Washington: The Alban Institute, 1995.

Foster, Charles R. *Embracing Diversity.* Washington: The Alban Institute, 1997.

Frensdorff, Wesley. *The Dream: A Church Renewed.* Cincinnati: Forward Movement, 1995.

Gore, Charles. *The New Theology and the Old Religion.* London: John Murray, 1908.

Goulder, Michael, ed. *Incarnation and Myth: The Debate Continued.* London: SCM Press, 1979.

Guiver, George. *Faith in Momentum: The Distinctiveness of the Church.* London: SPCK, 1990.

Harris, Mark. *The Challenge of Change: The Anglican Communion in the Post-Modern Era.* New York: Church Publishing Inc., 1999.

Hebert, A. G. *Liturgy and Society: The Function of the Church in the Modern World.* London: Faber and Faber Limited, 1961.

Hill, Jim, and Rand Cheadle. *The Bible Tells Me So: Uses and Abuses of Holy Scripture.* New York: Anchor Books/Doubleday, 1996.

Holloway, Richard, ed. *The Anglican Tradition.* Toronto: Anglican Book Centre, 1984.

Holmes, Urban T. *What Is Anglicanism?* Toronto: Anglican Book Centre, 1982.

Ingham, Michael. *Mansions of the Spirit: The Gospel in a Multi-Faith World.* Toronto: Anglican Book Centre, 1997.

Kew, Richard, and Roger White. *New Millenium, New Church: Trends Shaping the Episcopal Church for the 21st Century.* Cambridge: Cowley Publications, 1992.

———. *Toward 2015: A Church Odyssey.* Cambridge: Cowley Publications, 1997.

Kraemer, Hendrick. *A Theology of the Laity.* (reprint) Regent College, 1994.

The Lambeth Conference 1968 Resolutions and Reports. London: SPCK, 1968.

The Lambeth Report. London: SPCK, 1948.

Messer, Donald E. *Contemporary Images of Christian Ministry.* Nashville: Abingdon Press, 1989.

Morgan, Dewi. *1662 and All That.* London: A. R. Mowbray & Co. Ltd., 1961.

Platten, Stephen. *Augustine's Legacy: Authority and Leadership in the Anglican Communion.* London. Darton, Longman and Todd, 1997.

Ramsey, Arthur Michael. *The Gospel and the Catholic Church.* Cambridge: Cowley Publications, 1990.

Saul, John Ralston. *Reflections of a Siamese Twin: Canada at the End of the Twentieth Century.* Toronto: Penguin Books Canada, 1997.

Slocum, Robert Boak, ed. *A New Conversation: Essays on the Future of Theology and the Episcopal Church.* New York: Church Publishing Incorporated, 1999.

Solheim, James E. *Diversity or Disunity? Reflections on Lambeth 1998.* New York: Church Publishing Inc., 1999.

Stevenson, Kenneth, and Brian Spinks, eds. *The Integrity of Anglican Worship.* Edited by Kenneth Stevenson and Brian Spinks. Harrisburg: Morehouse, 1991.

Stuchbery, Ian. *This Is Our Faith.* Toronto: Anglican Book Centre, 1990.

Sykes, Stephen, and John Booty, eds. *The Study of Anglicanism.* London: SPCK/Fortress, 1988.

Sykes, Stephen. *The Integrity of Anglicanism.* New York: Seabury Press, 1978.

———. *Unashamed Anglicanism.* London: Darton, Longman and Todd, 1995.

Thompsett, Fredrica Harris. *We Are Theologians.* Cambridge: Cowley Publications, 1989.

———. *Living with History.* Cambridge: Cowley Publications, 1999.

The Truth Shall Make You Free. The Lambeth Conference 1988: The Reports, Resolutions & Pastoral Letters from the Bishops. London: Church House Publishing, 1988.

Westerhoff, Caroline. *Calling: A Song for the Baptized.* Cambridge: Cowley Publications, 1994. Foreword by John H. Westerhoff III.

White, Stephen Ross. *Authority and Anglicanism.* London: SCM Press, 1996.